❋ Paris at the End of the World ❋

Paris at the End of the World

THE CITY OF LIGHT DURING THE GREAT WAR, 1914–1918

John Baxter

HARPER ◑ PERENNIAL

NEW YORK • LONDON • TORONTO • SYDNEY • NEW DELHI • AUCKLAND

HARPER ⬤ PERENNIAL

All images from the collection of the author.

HarperCollins books may be purchased for educational, business, or sales promotional use. For information please e-mail the Special Markets Department at SPsales@harpercollins.com.

FIRST EDITION

Designed by Jennifer Daddio

Library of Congress Cataloging-in-Publication Data has been applied for.

BN 978-0-06-222140-7

7 18   OV/RRD   10 9 8 7 6 5 4 3 2 1

In the old days, men were absorbed in wars, filling all their existence with marches, raids, victories, but now all that is a thing of the past, leaving behind it a great void which there is so far nothing to fill: humanity is searching for it passionately, and of course will find it. Ah, if only it could be quickly!

ANTON CHEKHOV, *Three Sisters*, 1901

Contents

Contents

Contents

❋ Paris at the End of the World ❋

We sit in calm, airy, silent rooms opening upon sunlit
and embowered lawns, not a sound except of summer
and of husbandry disturbs the peace; but seven million
men . . . are in ceaseless battle from the Alps to the Ocean.
WINSTON CHURCHILL

*T*he first blow fell on Paris at 7:18 a.m. on March 21, 1918, interrupting the calm of a spring morning.

As its concussion echoed over the roofs, residents came to their front doors and stared at the sky. Was it another accident, like that of the previous January, when an ammunition dump in Courneuve blew up, shattering windows across the city?

People living close to the Canal Saint-Martin knew better. A crater had appeared in the wide stone towpath where horses usually dragged barges into the city. They assumed a German bomber had made an audacious solo raid, the pilot fleeing to the safety of his army's trenches that zigzagged across France from Belgium to the Swiss border.

Everywhere, Paris displayed dispiriting evidence of its vulnerability to aerial attack. Paper tape crisscrossed shop windows, and the lower portions of most monuments were heaped with sandbags. More bags blocked the doors of such great churches as Notre Dame de Paris. Wooden braces protected priceless stained glass.

Hoping to lure bombers away from the city, the army was constructing a fake Paris in the sleepy satellite town of Maisons-Laffitte, where a stretch of the Seine resembled the river as it ran through the capital. It included plywood replicas of the Arc de Triomphe and the Opéra, false train tracks, and facsimiles of such industrial suburbs as Saint-Denis and Aubervilliers. Ingenious lighting and translucent paint created the effect of light shining through the dirty glass of factory roofs.

The second blast, coming only fifteen minutes after the first, dispelled the theory of a high-flying bomber. When a third shell landed fifteen minutes after that, panic gripped Paris. Could a German fifth column be responsible? The labyrinth of underground stone quarries that honeycombed the hills of Montparnasse on the southern edge of the city offered plenty of hiding places. Maybe spies had set up a clandestine battery. This theory didn't survive the first examination of shrapnel fragments. The shells that materialized from a clear sky each fifteen minutes didn't come from either bombs or aircraft but from a cannon. Parisians with long memories recalled the siege of 1871 when Prussian artillery pounded portions of the city to rubble. Now, once again, a German gun of frightening power was zeroing in on Paris.

Forty miles northeast, where a bulge in the line of trenches brought the German positions closest to the city, engineers had been busy for weeks on the slopes of Mont de Joie, near the village of Crépy. Under cover of the forest, they constructed a railway spur line and a deep concrete emplacement—a nest for the greatest internal engine ever devised by man.

The barrel of the *Paris-Geschütz*, the Paris Gun, was as tall as a ten-story building. Each explosive charge was ten feet long. With the railway truck on which it stood, the gun weighed four hundred tons. Eighty men were needed to man it—sailors, not artillerymen, since long-barrel precision gunnery was the jealously guarded province of the *Kriegsmarine*. Each shot expended the power of nine million horses in a gush of orange smoke and flame. The 228-pound projectile left the barrel at a mile a second. Within a minute and a half, it had climbed twenty-four miles, to the edge of space. Three minutes after firing, the shell plunged into a street, a theater, a school, or a church.

The gun wasn't hard to find. Once the French realized that its shells fell along a single line, pinpointing its location became a matter of simple ballistics. What followed was a game of hide-and-seek, the French bombing and shelling the area around Crépy, the Germans laboriously shifting the gun to new emplacements and moving other units into the area to confuse aerial spotting.

French government propagandists encouraged magazines and newspapers to convey an image of a tranquil

The Paris Gun—range: 40 miles

Paris going about its business; illustrations showed groups of women working on embroidery by a window and concierges chatting on the sidewalk while children played nearby. André Lefèvre, an engineer in the city government, pointed out that "serious results from long-range guns were unlikely, as they were worn out after 80 or 100 shots." In fact, the barrels of this weapon were sent back to the Krupp factory after only sixty-five firings.

Though it inflicted only modest damage, the *Paris-Geschütz* taught Paris it was not exempt from war. Penance for this sin of omission was due, and soon paid. Seventy-one people died after a direct hit on the Bolivar métro station. On March 29, 1918—Good Friday—a shell plunged through the roof of the church of Saint-Gervais, in the very heart of the Marais, one of the city's oldest districts. It killed eighty-eight people and injured seventy-eight—the worst civilian casualties of the war. Next day, all Paris churches closed. Forced underground, the pious worshipped like early Christians, in cellars and catacombs. On Sundays in May and early June children in white veils and suits filed into basements, including that of the Bon Marché department store, to receive their First Communion.

The French 75—range: six miles

Before the Germans retired the weapon, it had fired 367 shells, killing 256 people and wounding 620—by trench standards a small loss, but of far greater damage psychologically. Parisians had believed intelligence, wit, and style could protect them from the worst effects of the war. Now they saw that these had the evanescence of a soap bubble. The grace of the *belle époque* had ended. The madness of *les années folles* was about to begin.

1

Two Men in Silk Pajamas

*He had burned several times to enlist. Tales of great
movements shook the land. They might not be distinctly
Homeric, but there seemed to be much glory in them. He
had read of marches, sieges, conflicts, and he had longed
to see it all. His busy mind had drawn for him large pictures extravagant in color, lurid with breathless deeds.*

STEPHEN CRANE, *The Red Badge of Courage*

In the bleak midwinter of 1916, General Douglas Haig, commander of the Allied armies in Europe, visited the Flanders front to unveil his plans for a spring offensive against the Central Powers of Germany and Austria.

He made his visit at a black time. In July of 1915, his attempt to break through the German lines had ended in slaughter. Believing that his men would take the enemy trenches without much trouble, he ordered them to advance standing upright, bayonets fixed. Within a few seconds, most were scythed down by fire from machine guns, a weapon Haig thought "much over-rated."

The British and French, supported by Canadian, Indian, and Australian volunteers, suffered 420,000 casualties during this campaign, 60,000 on the first day. The French alone lost 200,000 men and the Germans nearly 500,000 before the fighting halted in November for the winter and the war froze into stalemate.

To outline his plans for 1917, Haig called a conference of commanders. Few large buildings survived in the forward areas, but his staff found an intact château near the Belgian town of Nieuwpoort.

They didn't know it was already occupied.

*D*uring the first weeks of the war, Polish countess Misia Sert, one of the most fashionable hostesses in Paris, persuaded General Joseph-Simon Gallieni, the military governor, to authorize a private ambulance service. She would fit out the delivery vans of couturiers Paul Poiret and Jean Patou, which were sitting unused since all their staff had been drafted to make uniforms.

Poiret, before he left to create a new greatcoat for the army, designed an outfit for Misia's group: dark blue, gold buttons, collar flared, jacket theatrically skirted. His best illustrator, Paul Iribe, also joined Sert but preferred his own version of protective clothing: a deep-sea diver's suit, complete with solid brass helmet.

Other recruits included the young poet Jean Cocteau, a regular at Sert's salon in her Quai Voltaire apartment, overlooking the Seine and the Louvre. Cocteau recognized their motivation as less compassion than curiosity. The curtain was about to go up on the greatest first night of the century, more sensational even than the 1913 premiere of Igor Stravinsky's *Rite of Spring*, and they were determined to have front-row seats. "They were going behind the scenes of the drama," he wrote of the group. "They were like music-lovers in the dress circle listening to Stravinsky, leaning over the dark stalls."

For two years, Cocteau crisscrossed the war zone with Sert's group, then joined another formed by Count Etienne de Beaumont, famous for the costume balls at which he often appeared in elaborate drag. They fluttered behind the lines like butterflies, distributing cigarettes, candy, and other treats to the troops, and occasionally, though they had no medical training, ferrying casualties back to dressing stations. The much they

Jean Cocteau in Paul Poiret uniform

saw that was horrible made them more anxious than ever to think about something else.

In December 1916, they arrived in the area near Nieuwpoort, located a surviving château, and commandeered the best rooms. After a leisurely bath, the two men spent the afternoon trying on their most exquisite outfits, choosing finally two pairs of colorful silk pajamas. Scented, rouged, and powdered, with bracelets jingling at ankles and wrists, they descended to the salon, expecting to dine in solitary elegance—only to find General Haig and the entire high command huddled over maps spread out on the largest table.

For a frozen moment, rival visions of war stared at one another.

On one side, two exemplars of the Parisian way of life—theatrical, sophisticated, sensual. On the other, a humorless disciplinarian who embodied the puritan values of duty, country, service.

Cocteau and Beaumont excused themselves and crept back to their rooms to giggle at the looks on the staff officers' faces, while the "real" soldiers, shaking their heads in disbelief, returned to the business of planning death.

How could two such radically opposed cultures fight

Count Etienne de Beaumont

on the same side? What was the nature of the civilization they were battling to preserve?

And what was my paternal grandfather, William Archie Baxter, of Burrawang, New South Wales, doing in the middle of it?

Well, it was that kind of a war.

2

An Ice Cream War

The War That Will End War

H. G. WELLS, title of a book, 1914

In the summer of 1914, while all of Europe was on holiday, German troops flooded through Belgium, across the sand dunes and salt marshes of Flanders, and into northern France. Only a desperate counterattack by the French and British halted them at the river Marne, forty miles from Paris. France was saved by the city's military governor, General Gallieni, who rushed reinforcements to the battle in a fleet of taxis.

Until the armistice of November 1918, the so-called western front, a double line of trenches separated by a no man's land of barbed wire and mud, zigzagged from the English Channel to the Swiss border. The phrase *im Westen nichts Neues*—literally, "in the west, nothing new"—became so familiar to Germans that Erich Maria

Remarque used it as the title of a best-selling novel, published in English as *All Quiet on the Western Front*.

The narrow gaze of the cinema has left us with an eye-level vision of this war: a few yards of muddy ground, pitted with shell craters, swept by machine gun fire. Asked to describe the sector where he won his Medal of Honor, Sergeant Alvin York said, "I occupied one space in a fifty-mile front. I saw so little it hardly seems worthwhile discussing it."

Even strategists couldn't grasp the totality of this troglodyte warren, almost five hundred miles long and often miles across. Jean Cocteau called it "an incredible labyrinth of corridors, roads and underground galleries." Wilfred Owen arrived at the front for the first time after "a march of three miles over shelled road, then nearly three along a flooded trench"—flooded because large parts of the front were below the water table.

Douglas Haig's description of preparations for his 1917 "big push" hints at the scale of the world's first industrial war.

Vast stocks of ammunition and stores of all kinds had to be accumulated. Many miles of new railways—both standard and narrow gauge—and trench tramways were laid. All available roads were

*improved, many others made, and long causeways
built over marshy valleys. Many additional dug-outs
had to be provided as shelter for the troops, for use as
dressing stations for the wounded, and as magazines
for storing ammunition, food, water, and engineering
material. Scores of miles of deep communication
trenches had to be dug, as well as trenches for
telephone wires, assembly and assault trenches, and
numerous gun emplacements and observation posts.
Many wells and borings were sunk, and over one
hundred pumping plants installed. More than one
hundred and twenty miles of water mains were laid.*

With northern France cut off from its industries and
farms, everything had to come from Britain, its dominions, and the Americas. Most of it poured through the
port of Le Havre, at the mouth of the river Seine. In the
area between the front and the English Channel, farms,
villages, whole towns disappeared under an avalanche
of goods, equipment, animals, people, and the materials
to feed them. One supply center alone covered twelve
square miles. A twenty-five-mile area from the front to
Amiens became a military town, fed by new roads lined
with shell dumps and encampments.

From the front, hundreds of supply lines snaked back

to the Channel. Traffic in that direction was mainly the wounded and dead. Stretcher bearers carried casualties to dressing stations where doctors decided who justified treatment and who could not be saved. The fortunate won evacuation to the hospital port of Etaples, and thence to Britain for care and convalescence.

Sixty-five million men and women fought in what is variously called the First German War, *la guerre de '14,* the Great War, the European War, and World War I. The French, the Americans, the British, and their allies from the dominions, Australia, India, and Canada,

Troops of the Allied armies, Paris, 4 July 1916

lost 9,407,136 soldiers and civilians; the Austro-German Central powers, 7,153,241: 5 percent of their combined populations. Just as many more were wounded.

Some lived that war in blood and mud. Others ate ice cream.

The slaughters of the Somme, Belleau Wood, and Verdun can obscure the fact that, for each combatant who endured these horrors, just as many never fired a shot. They hauled freight, shuffled papers, nursed the wounded, buried the dead, wrote requisitions, drew maps, cooked meals, wrangled horses and mules, or, in the pungent phrase of General George Patton about a later war, "shoveled shit in Louisiana."

My father's father, Archie Baxter, belonged to this army of the unremarkable. He volunteered in Sydney in May 1916 to serve in the Australian Imperial Force and arrived in Le Havre at the end of that year. The war ended in November 1918 and he returned home early in 1919. He was never promoted above private, won no medals, earned no commendations.

What happened to him during those two years? Nobody in our family knew—except that the experience left him somehow harmed. Everyone agrees that for the rest of his life, he remained troubled and dissatisfied, haunted by memories of France.

3

Poetry and Pity

Ancient and Unteachable, abide—abide the Trumpets!
Once again the Trumpets, for the shuddering ground-
swell brings
Clamour over ocean of the harsh, pursuing Trumpets—
Trumpets of the Vanguard that have sworn no truce with
Kings!

RUDYARD KIPLING, *The Old Issue*

A century of myth-making has left us with a one-sided vision of the Great War. It often seems a slow-motion horror story, an opera of mud and blood, performed to a musical score one part "Land of Hope and Glory," one part "Mademoiselle from Armentières."

In fact, the war was less an opera than an opera house, even a score of them, with only a few of their stages presenting *The Trenches of Flanders*. Others played epics of love, sacrifice, crime, courage, beauty, horror, and cowardice. It was a culture, an industry; in the phrase of social historian John Brophy, "an enormous institution, with the prestige of a barbaric religion."

Just as poppies bloomed in Flanders earth, plowed by artillery and fertilized with blood, art fed on war. Wilfred Owen tried to distance himself from the realization that his best work flowed from carnage. "I am not concerned with poetry," he wrote stiffly. "My subject is war, and the pity of war. The poetry is in the pity."

Not all poets agreed. Though Owen's work and that of Edward Thomas, Siegfried Sassoon, and a few others earned them the label "the war poets," they were only a handful of those who wrote about the war, and a minority in doing so negatively. Magazines and newspapers of the time were awash with belligerent and patriotic doggerel celebrating the rightness of the conflict and the nobility of sacrifice—or rather Sacrifice, since the ennobling by capitalization of such concepts as Death and Honor runs through the rhetoric of the period like the murmur of an organ voluntary at a funeral. Sheep May Safely Graze.

Mediocrity was relieved by an occasional gifted voice. One of these belonged to the American Alan Seeger. His best-known poem, "I Have a Rendezvous with Death," though not immune from high serious-ness, is sincerely felt. While conceding that he'd prefer to die in comfort, "deep pillowed in silk and scented down," the poet accepts that Duty may dictate other-wise.

But I've a rendezvous with Death
At midnight in some flaming town,
When Spring trips north again this year,
And I to my pledged word am true,
I shall not fail that rendezvous.

Seeger kept his rendezvous in 1916, dying in action with the French Foreign Legion.

In one of the most quoted of all war poems, "In Flan-ders Fields," a Canadian doctor, John McCrea, some-what vaguely related the poppies of Flanders to a need to honor the dead by fighting on.

Take up our quarrel with the foe:
To you from failing hands we throw
The torch; be yours to hold it high.
If ye break faith with us who die
We shall not sleep, though poppies grow
In Flanders fields.

Tenuous or not, the connection of the poppy and World War I proved durable. We still buy and wear paper poppies to signify remembrance.

*O*f all these affirmative voices, the finest belonged to Rupert Brooke. A literary comet, effortlessly talented, Brooke was also physically alluring in the willowy and androgynous way that is archetypically English; fellow poet W. B. Yeats called him "the hand-

Rupert Brooke

somest young man in England." Brooke found the prospect of war positively elating. To him, it

caught our youth, and wakened us from sleeping,
With hand made sure, clear eye, and sharpened
power,
To turn, as swimmers into cleanness leaping.

Had he experienced combat, he might have changed his mind, but he became one of the thirty million who never had the chance. Though he did die in uniform, it wasn't in the trenches but on a troop ship off the Greek island of Skyros, and not from a bullet but from an infected mosquito bite. (In listing war's aspects, one shouldn't neglect farce.)

If there was a joke, however, it wasn't on Brooke. The monument to the war poets in Poets' Corner of Westminster Abbey, which he shares with Owen, Sassoon, Robert Graves, and a few other veterans, may bear Owen's quote about the poetry being in the pity, but it was Brooke's work that sold in the millions, continued to do so for decades after his death, and is today better known than that of his compatriots.

How much more consoling than the bitterness of Owen was Brooke's "The Soldier":

If I should die, think only this of me:
That there's some corner of a foreign field
That is forever England.

His sentiments were echoed by Philip Gibbs, a British novelist who became a war correspondent. Like many, Gibbs saw war as a cure-all: in his case a corrective to the pettiness of party politics. Of the week hostilities began, he noted approvingly that "the leaders of the nation abandoned their feuds. Their blood thrilled to old sentiments and old traditions which had seemed to belong to the lumber-room of history, with the moth-eaten garments of their ancestors."

Britain's poet laureate of the day, Robert Bridges, agreed. "Britons have ever fought well for their country, and their country's Cause is the high Cause of Freedom and Honour. We can therefore be happy in our sorrows, happy even in the death of our beloved who fall in the fight; for they die nobly, as heroes and saints die, with hearts and hands unstained by hatred or wrong."

Gibbs, Bridges, and Brooke could speak of war in abstractions—Freedom and Honor—because they didn't know its reality. If the public visualized war, it was the campaigns in Africa against the Boers and Zulus: militarily speaking, walks in the park. At Omdurman in the Sudan in 1898, 25,000 British and Egyptian troops, each man armed with a modern rifle, faced 52,000 spear-carrying, sword-waving warriors under their fanatical leader the Mahdi. The Sudanese lost 10,000 killed, the British 47.

No war had been fought on European soil since the Franco-Prussian conflict of 1870–1871. During the subsequent forty years at peace, professional armies had shrunk. Troops were aging and sketchily trained, their equipment out of date, duties reduced to ceremonial appearances, "maneuvers," or keeping order during riots and natural disasters.

The battles between France and Prussia had been as formal as those between toy soldiers on a nursery floor. War was thought of as a show. During the American Civil War, the citizens of Washington streamed out to watch General George McClellan defend the city. In 1854, British commanders and their guests ate a picnic on a hillside as they watched the Light Brigade charge the Russian guns at Balaclava.

Young men yearned for war as a chance to prove their courage. American writer Malcolm Cowley, who served as an ambulance and explosives driver in France, believed the risk of death sharpened the senses and stimulated creativity.

*The war created in young men a thirst for abstract
danger, not suffered for a cause but courted for itself;
if later they believed in the cause, it was partly
in recognition of the danger it conferred on them.
Danger was a relief from boredom; a stimulus to
the emotions, a color mixed with all others to make
them brighter.*

*There were moments in France when the senses
were immeasurably sharpened by the thought of
dying next day, or possibly next week. The trees
were green, not like ordinary trees, but like trees
in the still moment before a hurricane; the sky was
a special and ineffable blue; the grass smelled of
life itself; the image of death at twenty, the image
of love, mingled together into a keen, precarious
delight. Danger made it possible to write once more
about love, adventure, death.*

Once Douglas Haig predicted in August 1914 that
the Allies would defeat Germany in a matter of months,
boys rushed to volunteer, concerned the war would end
before they'd had their adventure. All over the world,
cuirassiers, uhlans, dragoons, and light horsemen
brushed off their uniforms and groomed their horses.
They could already see themselves thundering toward

The illusion of heroism

the enemy, sabers leveled, helmet plumes flying, silver breastplates gleaming.

*B*ut it's where the capitalization ends—where War becomes just war and Death simply death; where this amateur war, a war of imagination and expectation, the ice cream war, intersects with the reality of mustard gas and the machine gun—that one glimpses its transformative effects.

Nowhere was this more true than in Paris.

4

Jean

In Paris, everybody wants to be an actor; nobody is
content to be a spectator.

JEAN COCTEAU

*E*very war has its stars: men and women who, whatever their military importance, seize the imagination. Few are conventionally heroic. The brave don't last. They die in combat, taking their stories with them. Those who survive are often not so much courageous as cunning, self-serving, and skilled at self-promotion. Lionized out of proportion to their achievement, they and their experiences are exaggerated and falsified in the interests of patriotism, recruitment, or profit.

Because there had been no European war for forty years, the conflict of 1914–1918 produced a parade of heroes and heroines. American marksman Alvin York, fliers Eddie Rickenbacker and "Red Baron" Manfred von Richthofen, executed British nurse Edith Cavell, the poets Wilfred Owen and Rupert Brooke, and T. E. Lawrence, "Lawrence of Arabia," all became household names, embodying the experience of war as much in what they said and wrote as in any physical heroism. Members of the Australian and New Zealand Army Corps and the Australian Imperial Force were more self-effacing, While honoring a few examples of self-sacrifice, such as the efforts, finally fatal, of Jack Simpson and his donkey to save the wounded at Gallipoli, they took more satisfaction in the "spirit of Anzac," a collective capacity to endure.

Stars on the French side were more rare. Joseph Joffre, commander of the French army, wasn't star material. Fat and waddling, with a bushy white mustache, "Papa" Joffre resembled Colonel Blimp, the symbol of an antiquated officer class invented during World War II by cartoonist David Low. General Gallieni's imagination and audacity saved Paris and, many would argue, won the war, but he was sick and in retirement before war began and died before it ended. Philippe Pétain, defender of the fortress of Verdun in one of the most costly battles of the war, initially entered the pantheon, despite a manner that chilled many. They were not disappointed when he died in disgrace after agreeing to lead the Nazi puppet government of occupied France during World War II.

After the generals, the best candidates for fame were its aviators, dashing cavaliers of the sky such as Jean Mermoz, Georges Guynemer, and Roland Garros. And then such improbable outsiders as Jean Cocteau.

For an example of the brilliance, the creativity, the joie de vivre of Paris at the beginning of the twentieth century, look no further than Jean Maurice Eugène Clément Cocteau.

In 1914 he was twenty-five, a slim, chic, opinionated gay man, fox-faced and frighteningly alert, with a prodigious talent that he survived to exercise for another fifty years. "He was a maestro of every conceivable form," enthused one critic after his death in 1963. "He wrote poetry, fiction, drama and criticism, directed several films, went round the world in eighty days, even played the drums in a Parisian night club." He was also an accomplished artist, his signature image the high-browed pouting profile of a butch young stud, a fantasy Orpheus whose reality he would discover in the actor

Jean Marais, destined to become his star, lover, and heir.

The limelight and the darkness at its edge were Cocteau's natural environment. When he was ten, his father committed suicide. His mother was absent for long periods. The grandparents who raised him explained she was an actress, and often on tour. It wasn't until he was twenty that Jean, looking through some photographs of the Saint-Lazare prison, recognized her among the inmates. A kleptomaniac, she served a number of sentences for petty theft.

A longtime addict of opium, Cocteau knew the Paris underworld, and applauded the pulp writers and filmmakers who created such glamorous thieves and avengers as Fantomas, Judex, and Arsène Lupin. Defying the fashion for elegant aestheticism, he found sexual partners in the demimonde—sailors, sportsmen, teenage runaways. He helped manage the career of boxer and tap dancer "Panama" Al Brown, and rescued the young Jean Genet, a gifted writer but a thief, by hiring the best lawyers to save him from prison. As a young man, he also joined the group that waited with a bath of warm water in the wings of the Ballets Russes. When Vaslav Nijinsky staggered offstage, exhausted after having mesmerized audiences in *L'Après-midi d'un Faune* or *Le Spectre de la Rose*, they stripped off his sweat-soaked costume and sponged him down—as much, it seems, for their pleasure as for his.

When Cocteau signed up for Misia Sert's ambulance service, he was already a regular at her salon. In the way she drew the most brilliant men and women of Paris to her afternoon soirees, Misia, beautiful, voluptuous, bisexual, and rich, reminded him of the bird trainers who showed off their disciplined flights of swallows in the Luxembourg Gardens. "Angels seemed to fly around her like birds round a *dresseur d'oiseaux*," he wrote.

She was painted by Renoir and by Toulouse-Lautrec, who doubled as barman at her salon. Guests included composer Maurice Ravel, who dedicated works to her, couturier Coco Chanel, who became her lover, and Marcel Proust, for whom she inspired a character in *A la Recherche du Temps Perdu*. Many in her circle first heard of the war when a late guest burst in with news of Austria invading Serbia. He was shushed until Erik Satie had finished the premiere performance of his *Three Pieces in the Form of a Pear*.

When Misia heard the news of Sarajevo, she said, "What luck! Oh God, if only there really is a war." Dashing into the street, she was swept up in the general euphoria.

*I suddenly found myself perched on a white horse
riding before a cuirassier in gala uniform, round
whose neck I had wound a wreath of flowers. The
general excitement was such that this situation
did not for a moment strike me as being strange.
The cuirassier, the horse and the crowd were not
astonished either, for the same spectacle could
be seen throughout Paris. Flowers in wreaths,
bunches, bouquets and loose, were being sold on
every street corner, and a moment later you found
them on the kepis of the soldiers, on the end of
their bayonets or behind their ears. Everybody
kissed, sang, cried, laughed, trampled each other,
hugged each other; we were filled with compassion,
generosity, noble feelings, ready for any
sacrifice, and, as a result of it all, wonderfully,
unbelievably happy.*

The same spontaneity permeated Misia's ambulance
service. In *Thomas the Imposter*, Cocteau's novel about
the experience, he parodied her as the scatty Princess
de Bormes. "Danger was in fashion and the calm was
killing her," he wrote of her restlessness at the outbreak
of war. "The Princess is moved less by patriotism than
a sense that something is going on from which she is

barred. This fearless woman listened to the cannon like those who listen to the orchestra outside a concert hall to which the door-keeper will not admit them."

During the first days of the war, Cocteau shared the general enthusiasm. For such intellectuals as himself and the American writer Malcolm Cowley, ambulance work was mostly a giggle. Any risk of injury and death appeared remote, even exciting. As Winston Churchill said of being a correspondent during the Boer War, "Nothing in life is so exhilarating as to be shot at without result." Cowley and members of his crew darted out from cover in the middle of an artillery barrage to grab bits of shrapnel. "We were seeing a great show, collecting souvenirs of death, like guests bringing back a piece of wedding cake or a crushed flower from the bride's bouquet."

Black humor titters through Cocteau's evocation in *Thomas the Imposter* of a typical trip with a volunteer ambulance unit.

Madame Valiche opened the door.
"Ten minutes halt. Refreshments! All change!"
"Where are we?" asked Clemence, still half asleep.
Guillaume jumped out of his dream onto the

road. "We are at M———, *fair princess, and the*
casualties are shouting that they are glad of it."

Indeed, *a strange moaning sound came through*
the cold night, curses and banging on the partitions.

"They are in pain," *said Clemence.* "The road
is full of potholes."

"That didn't stop you sleeping. And it's for their
own good. We're taking them to bye-byes. They
don't know their luck."

A poilu *by Theophile Steinlen*

Cocteau posed in his Poiret uniform against the sand dunes of the Belgian coast and was snapped, smirking, next to a privy labeled *WC Réservé au Génie*—"Toilet Reserved for Engineers." (*Génie* also means "genius," a title Jean didn't doubt he deserved.) His descriptions of the wounded show a callous aestheticism, as if an awareness of beauty insulated him from pity and horror. Recruits mown down by machine guns were "poor flowering flesh; young trees, uprooted in the mud." Of a young gunner dying of blood poisoning, he imagined how "gangrene must have crept over him like ivy over a statue."

*I*n Paris, Cocteau patronized a public bathhouse where one of the twelve bathrooms, for the pleasure of wealthy voyeurs, was fitted with a one-way mirror. At the front, he loitered near the showers where the *poilus*, or "hairy ones," as common soldiers were known, took their first full wash in weeks. Among them were Zouaves, recruited from France's colony, Algeria. Malcolm Cowley saw these troops as simply "huge men with blue-black faces, pink eyeballs and white teeth," but to Cocteau they became sensual projections in negative of Antoninus, lover of the Roman emperor Hadrian and a popular subject of homoerotic statues. In his poem "The Shower," he wrote:

> *The negroes are Antoninus*
> *Seen in a black convex mirror.*
> *Ill, they become purple.*
> *They cough. Alas! Where are*
> *Your islands? Your crocodiles?*
> *Where are they?*

This mirror of war as beauty was shattered by his collision with Haig and his staff in the Flanders château. Shaken, he recoiled from the triviality of his ambulance excursions. "I left the war," he wrote later, "when I realized, one night in Nieuwpoort, that I was enjoying myself." He got a job in Paris editing a propaganda magazine, *Le Mot*—The Word—and it was there, in one of those improbable examples of six degrees of separation, that his path could have intersected, however briefly, with that of Archie Baxter.

Chocolate Soldiers

*But there's something about his bearing, something in
what he's wearing
Something about his buttons all a shine shine shine
Oh a military chest seems to suit the ladies best
There's something about a soldier that is fine fine fine.*
NOEL GAY, "Something About a Soldier"

After its defeat by the Prussians in 1871, France
constructed forts to bar the route from the east,
which, they assumed, any future German invader must
take. Colossal carbuncles of concrete, forty feet thick,
bristling with cannon, they were served by thousands
of men permanently quartered underground in miles
of tunnels.

Supporting them at ground level was a fast-moving
military machine geared to the style of fighting per-
fected by Napoleon Bonaparte. Its horse-drawn artil-

lery, mostly light 75 mm field guns, could move swiftly to meet any attack. Every Frenchman underwent two years' obligatory military service. This created a reservoir of trained troops, ready to be called up at the first whiff of hostilities. Each reservist received a *carnet de mobilization*, with details of where to report in the event of the war that many expected, even hoped would come.

For cavalry charges and infantry clashes in open country, France was well prepared. It knew nothing of long-range artillery, bombing, aerial reconnaissance, poison gas, the tank, and above all the machine gun. Even its colorful uniforms might have been designed to show contempt for modern warfare. Infantry wore a dark blue double-breasted tailcoat with brass buttons. The number of their regiment was embroidered on the collar. Baggy red trousers tucked into half-boots completed the outfit, which was topped with the kepi, a cylindrical cloth cap with a stiff brim: stylish but little protection against a bullet.

In forty-four years, nobody had ever worn this uniform under fire. Once they did, it proved embarrassingly visible, and the army hurriedly looked for a new design. The British, in the interests of consistency, urged them to adopt their khaki, but the French refused, for the very French reason that khaki resembled the brown fabrics

Fitted out for war

The poilu
uniform—
dangerously
visible.

favored by hunters. How embarrassing if an officer was mistaken for some farmer out with his shotgun to get a rabbit for the pot. They based their final choice, a pale "horizon blue," on the army's existing peacetime dress uniform, but French troops would always be more visible than the British in khaki, the Germans in gray, and the Americans whose dusty brown kit with cookie-like buttons earned them the label "doughboys."

It took many weeks for everyone to receive a new outfit. "This was the period when the old uniform, in the process of changing to the new, had become unrecognizable," wrote Cocteau. "Everyone wore it in his own way. And this cast-off kit, so comical in town, was magnificent in the armies—rank upon rank of ragamuffins." Some officers remained fanatically loyal to the old uniform. One raged at a private in mismatched gear and ordered him to replace his blue trousers with red ones from a corpse. When the man refused, he was shot.

Pockets of such fanaticism lingered, reminders of the reverence in which France held its army at the end of the previous century. British soldiers startled the French when, following a rumored gibe by the kaiser that they were "a contemptible little army," they began calling themselves "old contemptibles." No officer of the Grande Armée would accept such an adjective. To do so would demean not only him but the force and, by extension, the nation. When an artillery officer, Alfred Dreyfus, was wrongly condemned as a spy in 1894 and sent to Devil's Island, the high command hid its error for years, arguing that to reveal the injustice would un-

French officers toasting their tailor

dermine public confidence in the army. Novelist Emile Zola challenged this hypocrisy in his notorious broadside *J'Accuse*, and had to flee to England for his life.

Faithful to von Bismarck's ethic of "blood and steel," the German army dismissed the French as "chocolate soldiers," commanded by officers more concerned with creature comforts than with killing. In late September, as the western front stabilized along the Marne, a cartoonist for the Berlin-based comic magazine *Die Lustige Blätter*—The Funny Pages—showed monocled French cavalry officers relaxing in a château. Servants serve champagne and help them off with their high leather boots. One officer sings to another's piano accompaniment. Half-read novels litter the floor, and in the foreground is a lady's fashionable hat and hatbox. The caption sneered "These Frenchmen have decided not to take any notice of our advance." The French magazine that reprinted it meant to mock German arrogance, but anyone familiar with the high command in Paris knew the drawing wasn't far from the truth.

6

Taxi!

We need audacity, and yet more audacity, and always audacity!

GEORGES DANTON

From September 1914 to November 1918, Paris lived with war at the bottom of the garden. The trenches were as close as Times Square is to Bridgeport, Connecticut, or Santa Monica to Catalina Island. Commanders complained of inquisitive tourists wandering into the war zone, hoping for a closer look. In August 1914, American novelist Edith Wharton visited the border with Alsace and peeked over the mountain crest at the German batteries guarding it—after which, she explained, "we retreated hurriedly and unpacked our luncheon-basket on the more sheltered side of the ridge."

Flicking zeppelins

Parisians got used to the distant thud of artillery. Zeppelins flew over the city, but since the bombs dropped were small, one could shrug off the occasional crater. The cover on the issue for April 1916 of *La Vie Parisienne*, the *Playboy* of its day, shows an underdressed young woman flicking away zeppelins as if they're party balloons. Inside, the editors give fashion tips on what to wear in the air raid shelter. They recommend an ermine-trimmed evening coat over your nightgown. For head protection, they suggest borrowing a cap from your chauffeur.

In the absence of any recent experience, the war, both in Paris and at the front, was being improvised day by day. Which helps explain the episode of the taxis of the Marne.

When the Prussians defeated the French in 1871, they seized Alsace-Lorraine, the mineral-rich region along their border with France. Ever since, the loss of the province had maddened the French like an amputated limb that perversely continued to itch. On the Place de la Concorde, patriots draped in black a statue representing the eastern cities of Lille and Strasbourg, and laid wreaths there on state occasions. In Alsace itself, women discarded the red

In Alsace!

ribbons of their traditional headdress, vowing to wear only black ribbons until the German "theft" was corrected.

The moment France mobilized in August 1914, General Joffre put into force Plan XVII. Four of France's five armies, a total of 800,000 men, charged to the east, intent on reclaiming its lost territory. France's most popular picture magazine, *L'Illustration*, its equivalent of *Life*, led the issue of August 25 with a full-page drawing of a French officer, saber in hand, embracing a swooning Alsatian girl in her black headdress while his men surged past, trampling the spread-eagle standard of the Deutsches Reich. The caption was unequivocal. *En Alsace!* In Alsace!

Journalists were delirious. "I have pinned on my wall, opposite the end of my bed, the newspaper that carries in letters of triumph these remarkable words: 'The French in Alsace.' And I feed, without ever being satisfied, on this flamboyant headline. It has captured my heart. It pours on me like a refreshing wine. It drenches the totality of my soul."

In fact, Joffre had barely sighted Alsace when the Germans invaded Belgium and poured through on his flank. By the time that issue of *L'Illustration* went on sale, he was in full retreat. Adolphe Messimy, minister of war, called his senior general, Joseph-Simon Gallieni, out of retirement and offered him the thankless job of Paris's military governor. With it went command of the Sixth Division, all that remained to defend the city—not, emphasized Messimy, that Gallieni would actually need to fight, since defeat appeared inevitable. Joffre, ever cautious, planned to retreat across the Seine, if not farther, before he made a stand. Gallieni and his men should join him, leaving Paris to fend for itself.

But Gallieni was old school. Thin and tough as a riding crop, he'd graduated from France's West Point, the École Spéciale Militaire de Saint-Cyr. After a career mostly spent overseas, quelling rebellions in Madagascar and Indochina, he'd been offered command of the army in 1911. Though only in his late fifties, he turned it down, knowing he was dying of prostate cancer. The job went to "Papa" Joffre, whom he detested. "How fat he is," Gallieni sighed when he heard of the appointment. "He won't last three years." As it was, Joffre outlived him by fifteen years.

Gallieni took a day to think about Messimy's offer, then obeyed the call of duty that had ruled him all his life. The government, relieved to have found someone to cover its rear and its embarrassment, scuttled off to Bordeaux, at the other end of the country. Paris's street singers, the *Saturday Night Live* of the time, greeted this

General Gallieni

news with a parody of the national song, *La Marseillaise*. The original words, *Aux armes, citoyens / Formez vos bataillons*—To arms, citizens / Form your batallions— became *Aux gares, citoyens / Montez dans les wagons*—To the railroads, citizens / Board your wagons.

But abandoning Paris did not even cross Gallieni's mind. On September 2, as the Germans leaped the Marne and came within twenty miles of the capital, close enough for their scouts to see the Eiffel Tower, a poster appeared on walls all over the city.

Inhabitants of Paris.

*The members of the government of the Republic
have left Paris to give a new impetus to the defense
of the nation. I have received a mandate to defend
Paris against the invader. This mandate I will fulfil
to the end.*

Gallieni.

Almost immediately, the gamble paid off. By extraordinary luck, the French found the body of an officer from the staff of the German commander, Alexander von Kluck. A map in his pack showed that von Kluck intended to deviate from the invasion plan created by Count Alfred von Schlieffen. Instead of taking Paris, he would swing around the city, hoping to drive the French toward the Swiss border. But in doing so, he would open a thirty-mile gap on his flank. Gallieni badgered Joffre into joining the British in an attack into that breach— the thrust of a stiletto under the ribs.

From getting troops into Paris to defend it, Gallieni's problem changed to getting them out to where they were needed. He had called up the Seventh Division from reserve, but the men were stuck on the choked railway system. Rather than bring them into the bottleneck of Paris, he ordered the trains stopped at villages on the

One of the taxis of the Marne, preserved in the museum of the Hôtel des Invalides

outskirts. But how to transport thousands of men from there to the Marne?

In 1940, hundreds of pleasure craft and fishing boats would be mobilized to cross the English Channel and rescue British and French troops trapped on the beaches of Dunkirk. Twenty-six years earlier, Gallieni had a similar idea. Why not move the troops in private cars and taxis?

"That's brilliant, *mon général*," stammered an aide.

Believing, as did Ernest Hemingway, that "praise to the face is sheer disgrace," Gallieni harrumphed "*Eh bien, voilà au moins qui n'est pas banal!*" (Well, at least it's original!)

A call went out for automobiles and people to drive them. Racing cars, buses, and 150 of Paris's notoriously cranky cabbies assembled in front of the Hôtel des Invalides, the seventeenth-century veterans' hospital that had become army headquarters. Gallieni immediately sent them off in convoys, empty, to collect soldiers from villages such as Tremblay-lès-Gonesses, buried today under the runways of Charles de Gaulle Airport.

The red-painted Renault AG taxi was high and narrow, built to squeeze through congested streets. Its driver sat outside. Usually the compartment behind him carried only three passengers, but in 1914 five soldiers squeezed in, with their weapons and kit. They had a rough ride as the cabs jounced over dirt roads in the dark: headlights might have alerted the Germans. But astonishingly, it all worked, thanks in part to generous rations of *pinard*, the rough red wine the troops would rather drink than water.

In the course of two days, six hundred taxis ferried four thousand soldiers to the front. Their presence was decisive. The counterattack stopped the Germans dead, then forced them into retreat. It might have become a rout and ended the war, but Joffre lacked the men, the equipment, and the initiative to exploit his advantage. At the river Marne, forty miles from Paris, he dug in. So did the Germans. With their momentum lost and the Russians looming on their eastern border, they were effectively defeated. But the war would drag on for another four years. From time to time, one side created a "salient" or bulge in the line that the other forced back in place. When, occasionally, an assault broke through, the attackers had no plans for consolidating their success and were driven back to their trenches.

*I*n part because of its incongruous use of taxis, the first Battle of the Marne was never taken as seriously as the failed battles of the Somme and Ypres that followed. This was still the phony war, the one that could end by Christmas. Troops had not yet become numbed to absurdities, and could respond to them with a sense of fun.

One such incident took place on September 11 near the village of Bregy, as the French pursued the retreating Germans. A young artist, Georges Bruyere, reported it to his family in a letter.

We came up on a battalion of chasseurs taking a
break. Some were standing in a circle around an

object, and then, impossible as it was, we heard a
piano. What was it playing? A silly little waltz, one
of those waltzes you hear at neighborhood dances,
dear to the sentimental hearts of shop girls. But on
the tragic immensity of this plain where the shadows
were beginning to gather, it took on a character one
couldn't express.

As the tune suddenly changed, we realized it
was a mechanical piano. The melancholy waltz
was replaced by the craziest kind of polka from the
old days. Closing my eyes, I thought the plain was
spinning around me. But that wasn't it! The group
of soldiers was in motion. With grins on their faces,
they raised their arms, couples formed, and the
dance began.

Just as war didn't stop the French from staging an im-
promptu dance on the battlefield, it never succeeded in
stifling the commercial instinct, least of all in taxi drivers. As the front stabilized, they presented their bills:
forty miles to the Marne and back, and at night rates too.
And then there was the gasoline. . . . The ministry bar-
gained them down to 27 percent—including tip. War or
no war, some things about Paris were eternal.

7

The Taste of Transitoriness

*The lamps are going out all over Europe. We shall not
see them lit again in our time.*
EDWARD GRAY,
Britain's foreign secretary, 1914

I n 1914, it seemed impossible that anything, even
war, could impair the perfection of Paris. When
people of other nations desired the best in art and
music, food and drink, sex and sensation, fashion and
culture, they came here. History would call the period
from 1890 to 1914 *la belle époque*— "the beautiful age."

The languid compositions of Claude Debussy and
Maurice Ravel, sighs made music, soothed the air and
wooed the mind. Inspired by the swirls of vines and
tendrils, and of women's hair, the design style known
as *art nouveau*, "new art," emphasized that France was

the Woman of Europe and Paris therefore the Woman of France. The city basked in a golden glow—literally, since the introduction in 1828 of street lighting on the Champs-Elysées, its most fashionable avenue, made Paris the best-lit capital in Europe. Gas lamps rather than culture earned the title *la ville-lumière*—the city of light.

On this flood of sensation and creativity, fashionable Parisians bobbed in a bubble perfumed with private references and intimate relationships and inflated with talk. An Australian visitor in 1909 was enchanted by "the alert, vivacious faces of the people in the streets; from the shrug of the men's shoulders, the cut of their clothes and the careless swing of their canes; from the way the women carry themselves, and, above all, from the light-hearted drift and chatter about the cafés."

Conversation was, indeed, queen. But speaking French alone didn't win an entrée to this culture of insiders. One had to speak the French of the dinner table and salon, with its courtly compliments, private jokes, and classical citations, its gossip and scandal. As the novelist John Gregory Dunne wrote of Hollywood almost a century later, discourse in such cultures is "all context, shared references, and coded knowledge of the private idiosyncrasies of very public people." American novel-

Art nouveau by Alphonse Mucha

ist Edith Wharton, who remained in France throughout the war, wrote:

> *Everything connected with dinner-giving has an*
> *almost sacramental importance in France. The quality*
> *of the cooking comes first; but, once this is assured,*
> *the hostess' chief concern is that the quality of the*
> *talk shall match it. To attain this, the guests are as*
> *carefully chosen as boxers for a championship; their*
> *number is strictly limited, and care is taken not to*
> *invite two champions likely to talk each other down.*

In a society preoccupied with the moment, people talked and thought obsessively about memory and time. Its finest writer, Marcel Proust, spent his life recreating in lapidary detail the fashionable society of his youth.

Jean Cocteau, an opium addict, celebrated the drug's capacity to make time stand still. The nineteenth century had introduced man to only one entirely new sensation—speed. Opium was its necessary antithesis. "Everything one does in life," Cocteau wrote, "even love, occurs in an express train racing toward death. To smoke opium is to escape from the train while it is still

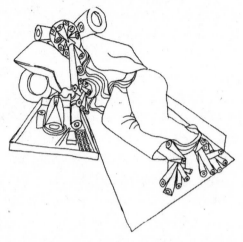

*A man made of opium. Cocteau as addict, drawn
by himself during detoxification. At the height of
his addiction, he smoked sixty pipes a day.*

moving. It is to concern oneself with something other
than life or death."

In 1900, Oscar Wilde, hiding in France after his release from jail, succumbed to meningitis in a hotel on
Paris's rue des Beaux Arts that was not only decorated in
appalling taste—"This wallpaper and I are fighting a duel
to the death. Either it goes," he said, "or I do"—but also
overpriced. "I am dying as I lived," he joked, "beyond my
means." That was true of France in general. Weakened by
lax government, financial mismanagement, and institu-

tional graft, the country was sliding toward bankruptcy. But that just made life in Paris more exhilarating.

To see the end approaching like a distant train but do nothing to step off the tracks has always held, for some intellectuals, a perverse appeal. In Paris during the French Revolution of 1789 and in Berlin and Vienna in 1933 under the threat of Nazism, artists and aristocrats felt the same delicious languor—Cocteau's "concern with something other than life and death."

In Austria during the early 1930s, the finest theatrical talent of his time, Max Reinhardt, ended each season of the Salzburg Festival with a midnight soirée at his château, Leopoldskron. As the horse-drawn carriages drew away at three or four in the morning, he would whisper to a few close friends, "Stay for an hour." The playwright Carl Zuckmayer recalled, "That hour often stretched on to five or six in the morning. Once, at a late hour, I heard Reinhardt say almost with satisfaction, 'The nicest part of these festival summers is that each one may be the last.' After a pause, he added, 'You can feel the taste of transitoriness on your tongue.'"

Not all Parisians were aristocrats and artists. Most never saw the *gratin*—the upper crust.

Historian Jean-Pierre Gueno has listed some of the concerns of ordinary people in the years leading up to the war; concerns that seldom make it into social histories, so seductive is the world of the *salon* and the *atelier*.

"It was the time of the Montmartre painters," he writes, "and the *Bateau-Lavoir*." The *Bateau-Lavoir* was a studio in an old Montmartre factory, shared by Picasso and Braque, and so named because in bad weather it creaked like the floating laundries moored along the Seine. It was the time of "the flooding of the Seine"—in 1910, the Seine overflowed and paralyzed the city for a month—"the passage of Halley's comet; the appearance of the first tangos; the first music halls; the inauguration of the Gaumont Palace [a cinema] and the Vél d'Hiv"—the Vélodrome d'Hiver, an indoor stadium that housed bike races, circuses, wrestling, and other sports, including events of the 1924 Olympic Games—"the theft of the *Mona Lisa*"—in August 1911, an Italian worker in the Louvre walked off with the Leonardo, smuggled it into Italy, and, a year later, gave himself up, along with the painting—"the end of the Bonnot gang"—an anarchist group that robbed banks between 1911 and 1913, pioneering the criminal use of automobiles; most members were imprisoned or executed in 1913—"the pub-

lication of *The War of the Buttons*"—Louis Pergaud's
1912 novel about gangs of village kids who begin by cutting buttons from rivals' clothes, then escalate to going
naked—"the meeting of Yvonne de Quiévrecourt and
Alain-Fournier under the trees of the Cours la Reine;
the edition of *Le Grand Meaulnes* that only just failed
to win the Prix Goncourt"—in 1905, Henri-Alban
Fournier fell in love with Yvonne de Quiévrecourt while
walking by the Seine; they never married, but she inspired him to write, as Alain-Fournier, his only novel,
which narrowly missed achieving France's highest literary honor—"the appearance of the first public telephone boxes; the electrification of the railways; the first
Michelin road maps; the fashion for peaked caps and
straw boaters; the invention of Esperanto."

This France was no less affected by the war—in
which, as it happens, both Louis Pergaud and Alain-
Fournier died. Although both *Le Grand Meaulnes* and
La Guerre des Boutons would become classics, filmed
repeatedly and never out of print, the France in which
they were set, of country romances and childhood
games, didn't survive. Neither did anarchy, the political
creed that drove the Bonnot gang and the Serbian as-
sassins who, indirectly ignited the war, nor Esperanto,
the synthetic language intended to break down barriers

between nations. Nobody was speaking Esperanto or preaching anarchy in the trenches of the Somme. Both had gone the way of boaters and bike races. Evil, as always, proved more durable. The Vél d'Hiv flourished. Under Nazi occupation, it became a holding center for French Jews about to be deported. In 1946, it reopened as a sporting venue and operated successfully until 1958.

8

Has Anybody Seen Archie?

O Muse! the causes and the crimes relate,—
What goddess was provok'd, and whence her hate;
For what offense the Queen of Heav'n began
To persecute so brave, so just a man;
Involv'd his anxious life in endless cares,
Expos'd to wants, and hurried into wars!

VIRGIL, *The Aeneid*,
translated by John Dryden

For two hundred years, the Baxters have been reluctant travelers. My ancestors arrived in Australia from Germany, Sweden, and Scotland during the nineteenth century—in some cases not without a struggle—and decided they'd gone far enough. None ever went back. My mother and father left Australia only once in their lives. In their eighties, they visited France to inspect our daughter Louise, the family's only grandchild. Having established to their satisfaction that such a rarity could exist, they returned home and never left again.

This tendency to put down roots and cling to them makes the experience of my grandfather, Archie Baxter, all the more puzzling. Not only did he spend three years in France between 1916 and 1919. He *volunteered* to do so.

Even more mysteriously, when he returned to Australia, he refused to rejoin his wife Stella, his daughter, and his son Jack, my father, nor return to his job as a grocery salesman. Instead, he rented a house in inner Sydney and started making and selling what our skimpy family records describe only as "condiments."

Almost inevitably, this enterprise failed. If there is such a thing as a business gene, the Baxter DNA conspicuously lacks it. Resignedly, Archie went back to his wife and children, and a dead-end job in the grocery trade. But nostalgia for Europe infected him like a disease. The rest of his life, he was tormented, it seems, by a desire to return to France, and in particular to Paris.

He scattered French words and phrases through his conversation, not troubling to explain why or to translate.

As a boy, my father memorized these. After Archie died, he continued to use them, though with little comprehension. I learned them too. *"Dans la cité des ténèbres,"* my father would mumble after three or four beers, *"je cherche la verité."*——In the city of darkness, I search for the truth.

What city? What truth? He never said. The words had become a mantra.

Another phrase was even more puzzling.

After he sold his shop, my father built a cabin in the garden behind his home in the Blue Mountains outside Sydney. Instead of the traditional names for such retreats, Mon Repos or Emoh Ruo (hint—spell it backwards), he chose a French phrase, or at least his own father's version of it. Hearing it repeatedly, my dad came to see it as the condensation of his father's hard-won wisdom, as well as his testament of despair. So significant did he find the words that he had a local carpenter cut out a phonetic approximation of them and hung it over the door of his retreat.

What Archie had seemed to mumble was *"San Fairy Ann."*

"But he meant *'Ca ne fait rien,'*" said my French wife, Marie-Dominique, when I told her this story. "In English, you would say, 'That doesn't matter,' or rather 'It means nothing.'"

"Yes. I know that. But why would Archie have found those words so important?"

She shrugged. "Everyone feels that way from time to time. It is *le malaise du temps*."

I doubted that anybody in Australia ever heard of *le malaise du temps*, the unease of our time, let alone suffered from it. If they did, they probably thought it was the flu. The French believe everything can be explained with reference to what obtains in France. So deeply ingrained is their love of the country, its culture and its language, usually lumped together as *la patrimoine*— heritage—that they don't understand how alien this can appear to foreigners, particularly to those who come from less sophisticated societies.

Even after a lifetime's exposure to French culture, I'd found relocating there a troubling and sometimes painful experience. How much harder for the American, British, Canadian, and Australian recruits, mostly uneducated, uncultured and naïve, who flooded into Paris between 1914 and 1918. Few people could have felt more lost, more in need of a friendly word, a loving hand. For them, Paris was literally "a city of darkness," where truth was not easily found.

9

The Photograph

What'll I do
With just a photograph
To tell my troubles to?
IRVING BERLIN, "What'll I Do?," 1923

When I was a child and we lived in an apartment next to the bakery in suburban Sydney, Grandfather Archie often visited us for Sunday lunch.

I remember him vaguely, in the way one does a person who disappeared from one's life when one was seven. He's indistinct, a scatter of impressions: bulky, white-haired, expressionless, monosyllabic, smelling of sweat, tobacco, and age. I was too young to ask the classic question, "What did you do in the war, Grandpa?" but he probably would not have answered. With a more recent

Archie in the 1930s—with his wife, Stella, and his daughter Maureen, and on Anzac Day

war only just ended, most Australians regarded the conflict of 1914–1918 as remote and irrelevant, best forgotten.

In time, I discovered that Archie volunteered for the First Australian Imperial Force in May 1916, when he was thirty-one, and sailed for France that October. I would never even have known this except that our own family, following Archie's death in 1947, moved into the house where he and my grandmother had lived and died.

A single-story cream-painted Victorian villa in solid Sydney sandstone, it stood behind a fence of spear-shaped iron railings on a hillside street of identical houses in the inner Sydney suburb of Leichhardt. My father and uncle inherited it jointly. Since housing was scarce, they decided to move in and share it. Disaster. Arguments between the families soon escalated into outright warfare. In the great tradition of political compromise, they partitioned the territory. Our family got the three front rooms, and my uncle the rest. Kitchen and bathroom were common ground. Any communication took place through third parties or via terse notes.

I blamed the house. From the start, it depressed me. I couldn't forget my grandmother's corpse laid out in her old bedroom, white hair a nimbus around her head, face set in the weary half-smile that was her most common expression in life. The mustiness of a century hovered in the high-ceilinged rooms with their plaster moldings and varnished picture rails. Bedside cabinets held those bits of medical equipment—chipped enamel, crumbling red rubber—that furnish props for the last years of the aged.

The parlor was dominated by a large framed black-and-white print of Millais' *The Two Princes Edward and Richard in the Tower, 1483*, showing the doomed boys, pale and long-haired, fearfully clutching one another as they await murder by Richard III. What sort of person hangs such an image on his wall? It said a good deal about Archie's state of mind. Even more sinister was a black cast-iron doorstop in the form of a grimacing hook-nosed Mister Punch. In every way—style, shape, weight—it was made to bash someone's head in.

Only my baby sister was unaffected by the house's brooding vibe. Finding the worn linoleum ideal for sliding, she rowed herself along on her diapered behind with a surprising turn of speed. We got used to her skimming down the hall and cornering expertly into the living room. Those of us with more weight, however, had problems. Dry rot was everywhere. Once, my foot broke through the boards, engulfing my leg to the thigh. The instant during which it dangled there, in what spider-infested dark I could only imagine, became a special horror I never forgot.

The musty closets and towering wardrobes in mahogany and oak hid tin trunks, rusty and dented, inside which were relics of Archie's war. One contained pieces of uniform, badges and buttons, and puttees in khaki wool. It also included a German military belt embossed with the slogan *Gott Mitt Uns*—God is with us. Our father recalled, expressionlessly, that it was with this belt that he had been beaten as a child.

Another disclosed more militaria, including a pistol, a few rounds of rifle ammunition, and a brown felt hat. Australia has no more potent military symbol than the slouch hat, which is still worn today. A leather chin strap keeps it at a casual tilt, or "slouch," toward the left ear. The brim is turned up on the right side and secured to the crown by a badge. Some regiments added a plume from that oddest of Australia's birds, the flightless ostrich-like emu. Though an English cartoonist suggested that Anzacs wore the hat with the brim turned up since it allowed them to press their cheeks closer to that of the girls they met, the hat had an iconic significance emphasized in a patriotic song of the 1940s.

> *It's a brown slouch hat with the side turned up, and
> it means the world to me.*
> *It's the symbol of our Nation—the land of liberty.*
> *And as soldiers they wear it, how proudly they bear
> it, for all the world to see.*
> *Just a brown slouch hat with the side turned up,
> heading straight for victory.*

We also found the photograph.
Most families have at least one such image.

Going to war, like getting married, was a rite of passage. It demanded a formal portrait. "Something to remember him by," murmured relatives, "Just in case . . ." When the soldier returned, it wasn't unusual to have another taken before he returned definitively to civilian life. ("You look so handsome in your uniform.") Certain studios offered a confidential service to families whose son or father died unphotographed. They supplied a man of similar build, wearing the correct uniform, to pose with the bereaved relatives. In the darkroom, his face was replaced, not always convincingly, with the dead man's features, taken from a snapshot.

As usual with studio portraits, the photographer posed Archie and Stella against a painted backcloth. Ironically, considering what I later learned of Archie's war service, it shows a scene in rural France. Almost hidden by a grove of trees and separated from them by a stone balustrade, a château in the style of the Second Empire stands complacently in a landscape straight out of Corot.

Archie, in full uniform, including tightly wound puttees and peaked cap, sits on a hard wooden chair. Stella stands behind him, one hand on his shoulder, the other on his arm. Wearing a wide plumed hat, ankle-length black dress, and small, round spectacles, she radiates will.

Did I imagine it or does she appear to be holding Archie down? And surely his expressionless stare and the clenched fists in his lap convey, more poignantly than any written or spoken word, the mute appeal, "Get me out of here!"

Our family was convinced that experiences in the trenches explained Archie's erratic postwar behavior. Some believed he'd been wounded. Others suggested shell shock—today's post-traumatic stress disorder.

My father hinted at a less medical reason. When I married Marie-Dominique and moved to Paris, he confided, with a significant wink, "If you see anyone on the streets who looks like you, the resemblance might be more than coincidence." Though I pressed him for details, he offered none. But the very thought that I might have unacknowledged uncles or aunts in France made the prospect of living in Paris even more enticing.

10

Strangers in Paradise

*As an artist, a man has no home in Europe
save in Paris.*
FRIEDRICH NIETZSCHE

Tourism began with the end of World War I. Before then, few people traveled far from where they were born. Emigration was a last resort, contemplated only in cases of cataclysmic social breakdown, such as the famine brought on by the 1845 Irish potato blight or the 1880s pogroms against Russian Jews.

The handful of Americans, Australians, Canadians, or Russians who came to Paris before 1914 did so for one of three reasons: they were rich, they were poor, or they had something to hide.

The rich were drawn to France as a flower is drawn to the sun. An American heiress or Russian princess would order her wedding dress and trousseau from such couturiers as Paquin, Worth, or Poiret and travel to Paris for fittings. At the same time, she might commission a set of silverware from Puiforcat or a service of Limoges porcelain, and perhaps acquire a French chef or ladies' maid.

While she did so, her father and fiancé would browse the art accumulated by successive monarchies and add to their own collections. If sportsmen, they watched thoroughbreds race at Longchamp, or hunted deer and pheasant in the forest of Rambouillet. At night, they ate and drank at Paris's restaurants or enjoyed the company of its women, the most beautiful in the world, and the most skilled at giving pleasure.

Another kind of hunter, or rather huntress, came to Paris hoping to acquire an aristocrat of her own. Watching throngs of heiresses cruise toward France aboard the Cunard and White Star liners, one wit christened them "the fishing fleet." Nothing flattered these nouveaux riches more than a European title. It put a shine on the millions earned in mining, railroads, or beer, while, to an impecunious French aristo, such a marriage could mean a new roof for the family château, a town house in Paris, a box at the Opéra, and a carriage to ride in the Bois de Boulogne.

A few such couples, after a while, even grew to like one another, but most exploited the marriage for all they could get, then bowed out. Anna Gould, daughter of railroad millionaire Jay Gould, and uncharitably compared to a chimpanzee in appearance, purchased Paul Ernest Boniface "Boni," Marquis de Castellane, Paris's handsomest though poorest bachelor. By the time they divorced in 1906, he'd reduced her fortune by $10 million—a modest price, she may have thought, for the right to call herself la Comtesse de Castellane.

The second category of foreigners exiled in Paris had little money, but they didn't feel they needed it. Anyone willing to subsist, cold and hungry, in a bug-infested garret while learning to write, paint, or compose could do so for longer in Paris than in any civilized city on Earth. In America or Australia, a person who preferred art to business was regarded with suspicion. But the French tolerated, even treasured, their bohemians. Nobody urged them to find respectable work; quite the reverse. In 1899, describing young painters studying at the many private art schools, an American wrote:

> *Students are the pets of Paris. They lend to the city*
> *a picturesqueness that no other city enjoys. So long*
> *as they avoid riots aimed at a government that may*

*now and then offend their sense of right, their ways
of living, their escapades, their noisy and joyous
manifestations of healthy young animal life are
good-naturedly overlooked.*

In Puccini's opera *La Bohème*, inspired by Henry Murger's *Scènes de la Vie de Bohème*, the students are so poor that Rodolfo, a novelist, has to burn the manuscript of a novel to keep warm. Mimi, the model with whom he falls in love, is dying of tuberculosis, a disease epidemic in the tenements where they lived. But at night they meet at Café Momus, where Musetta, a model who has hooked a rich lover, struts her good fortune. Hundreds of such students subsisted in Paris on a trickle of dollars, rubles, or yen sent from home—a situation that would rebound on them in 1914.

Between the rich and poor, but overlapping both, a third group chose Paris because it permitted them to enjoy pleasures which, back home, were illegal or disreputable.

Sex was everywhere. Prostitutes loitered along the boulevards and congregated in certain cafés and bars, the addresses of which were listed, along with the ladies' specialties, in the booklets called *guides roses*.

Wealthier sensualists patronized brothels. At Le

Chabanais, the most select and expensive whorehouse in France, if not the world, you could indulge your fantasies in opulently decorated rooms that imitated a tent in the Sahara or an Arctic igloo. The owners, a syndicate of wealthy sportsmen, most of them members of the snobbish Jockey Club, took pride in their establishment. They bought entire rooms from Paris's frequent exhibitions of exotic furniture and decoration and transferred them intact to the mansion on rue Chabanais. Toulouse-Lautrec decorated one room with images of centaurs.

Regular clients included Queen Victoria's portly son, Edward, Prince of Wales, the future King Edward VII. In contrast to his saintly ancestor, Edward the Confessor, Bertie was known as "Edward the Caresser." He liked to relax at Le Chabanais with his cronies as a girl splashed in a gilded bath filled with champagne. Periodically the men dipped out a glass and raised the kind of loyal toast never heard at Buckingham Palace.

Paris's permissive moral climate was just as encouraging to women. In Manhattan or Melbourne, lesbians had to hide their nature, but in Paris Sylvia Beach and Gertrude Stein lived openly with their companions and socialized at 20 rue Jacob, the home of railroad heiress Nathalie Clifford Barney. She even built a columned temple on the grounds, where she and her friends gathered in Greek robes to recite the poems of Sappho and make love, free of moral or legal restraints.

If you preferred pharmaceutical sensations, the "green fairy" of absinthe, flavored with wormwood, had a devoted following. Its drinkers shrugged off the threat of brain damage from impurities in the brewing process, a small price to pay for the "artificial paradises" celebrated in the poems of Charles Baudelaire.

Intellectuals and socialites preferred hashish from the cannabis plantations of France's North African colonies. No opium was more fragrant than that from the poppies of Annam and Tonkin, and Paris's *fumeries* competed to offer the most opulent décor in which to savor it. Ladies favored the drug dissolved in spiced alcohol as laudanum—the Prozac of the *belle époque*.

If you fancied a change, the more refined heroin and—the modish favorite—morphine, were freely available. Socialites carried their own hypodermics, ready to shoot up at supper parties in the hotels across the Place de l'Opéra. The most fashionable syringe, the Pravaz, could be made to order in platinum or gold and inlaid with precious stones as a gift for lover or wife.

Hard drug use wasn't confined to France. Although aspirin, as a synthetic, was available only on prescription, "natural" drugs such as cocaine, heroin, or opium could be bought legally at any pharmacy in the form of pills, gels, syrups, even teas. Harrods, London's most select department store, possessors of the royal warrant to supply goods to the royal family, sold vials of heroin gel, and a drug kit containing cocaine, morphine, syringes, and needles which it recommended to "sweethearts and mothers" as "a Welcome Present for Friends at the Front." The British government only restricted its sale when commanders complained of officers too stoned to go "over the top."

Though Paris encouraged those diversions known to other cultures as vices, in a city founded on fashion they seldom lasted longer than a season. No dismissal was more damning than the label *vieux jeux*—old games. As summer vacations ended in 1914 and people wandered back to Paris, its *jeunesse dorée*, gilded youth, looked around languidly for the next diversion.

But autumn 1914 brought no caravan from the Americas or Asia with an exciting cargo of new styles and ideas. Nothing would arrive to equal Sergei Diaghilev's Ballets Russes, which had sent ripples across the surface of painting, music, and *couture* in 1909. The great scandal of 1913, the premiere of *Le Sacre du Printemps*, would not be repeated. Instead, "old games" would continue to be played until their pleasure soured and staled. "Like a fruit," wrote Cocteau, "a short war might have grown and dropped from the tree, whilst a war prolonged for exceptional reasons, firmly attached to the branch, went on growing, ever presenting new problems and new lessons to be learnt."

11

Meeting at Plane Corner

*Chance furnishes me with what I need. I'm like a man
who stumbles; my foot strikes something, I look down,
and there is exactly what I'm in need of.*

JAMES JOYCE, on writing *Finnegans Wake*

Stories take on their own lives, drawing you along,
often oblivious, in their wake. So when I accepted
an invitation to a lunchtime lecture on antipodean food
at the Australian embassy, I wasn't thinking about my
grandfather's presence in Paris.

The lecture by a respected food historian was followed by a *coctel*, with canapés proposed by her and
cooked by the ambassador's own chef.

"There'll be meat pies," she confided, "and laming-tons. And even Iced VoVos."

Iced VoVos! Offering Proust a madeleine from Combray would have had just as electric an effect. These pink-frosted cookies were one of my childhood's treasured treats: islands of sweetness in the sludgy swamp of Australian cuisine.

As for the rest, I was in no hurry to be reintroduced to either meat pies or the lamington, a confection made by dipping stale cake in chocolate sauce and rolling it in desiccated coconut. Instead I drifted away from the post-lecture crowd into the exhibition area next door, where, by chance, two collections of photographs from World War I were on show.

One image immediately caught my eye. It showed an Australian and three French *poilus* excavating a pit in which to bury a bloated and stinking dead horse. Though one can't photograph a stench, the distaste on their faces and the fact that one man wore a gas mask told the story all too well. In the background, a leafless tree incongruously supported the skeleton of an aircraft. On that account, explained a caption, the troops called this Plane Corner.

The photograph captured one of those moments when war ceases to be a matter of brute forces in op-

position, and becomes, if only by accident, art. The man made anonymous by the gas mask, another's jaunty slouch hat, the bulk of the dead animal, the aircraft in a tree, gave to the image a quality of collage, as if someone had cut details from other photographs and juxtaposed them in a Max Ernst–like pastiche. André Breton conceived of surrealism while treating psychiatric casualties whose nightmares were more real than anything in the observable world. But sometimes, as in this photograph, daily existence achieved the strangeness of those tormented dreams. . . .

"John Baxter?" someone said at my elbow.

The man only came to my shoulder. His pale face, gray tweed jacket, and neatly pressed flannel trousers made him seem monochrome, a figure from one of these photographs. One could imagine him strolling along the rutted clay of the road to Plane Corner, glancing at the soldiers burying the horse, then stepping down into the room to join me.

"Peter van Diemen," he prompted.

"Of course." I took the thin hand. "It's been a long time."

The skin of his face, stretched tight across the skull, erased wrinkles and made his mouth look lipless. It twitched at the corners. Was that a smile or a grimace?

"You live here now?" I asked.

"Oh, yes. More than ten years. And you for longer, I think. Almost twenty?"

"Twenty-one."

He knew more about me than I did about him. But one expected no less. Peter van Diemen attracted information the way iron filings cling to a magnet. "The facts are out there," he told me once. "You just have to let them in." He would have made a perfect spy. *How did I know he wasn't?*

"My grandfather was here in 1916." I nodded toward the photograph. "He could easily have been one of these men."

"What was his regiment?"

"I don't know. In fact, I hardly know anything about his war service."

"Really?" Air sensing a vacuum could not have been more eager. "Well, if there is anything I can do . . ." He handed me a business card. "I'm retired, but still . . ." Again, that twitch of the lips. "The old fire horse, you know?"

Outside, I looked at the card. Just his name, with an address in the fourteenth arrondissement. Near the Santé Prison.

"So how was it?" Marie-Dominique asked when I got home.

"Oh, the lecture? Very good. But you'll never guess who I met. Peter van Diemen."

"The publisher from London?"

"Yes. We got talking about some World War I photos. He offered to help if I wanted to find out more about Archie. Military research was always his field. I'm quite tempted, actually."

Marie-Do closed one eye and scrunched up her face, as if looking at something in the middle distance and puzzling over its significance. I knew the expression. It indicated skepticism.

"Always remembering he's a murderer, of course," she said.

"Oh, yes," I said. "Always remembering that."

12

Master of War

I knew a man once did a girl in
Any man might do a girl in
Any man has to, needs to, wants to
Once in a lifetime, do a girl in.

T. S. ELIOT, *Sweeney Agonistes*

Peter and I went back a long way—to my first months in England. With my girlfriend of the time, I had rented a cottage in the Suffolk village of East Bergholt. Twice a week, I took the train to London and did the rounds of publishers, hoping one would commission the book I wanted to write about movie stuntmen.

Progress was slow, but, in time, one editor, though not enthusiastic himself, thought it might interest a colleague.

"Peter's our militaria man," he said. "I'll take you along."

Militaria? I couldn't see the connection, but I let myself be led to a tiny cluttered office at the end of a long corridor.

"John, meet Peter van Diemen."

Peter hadn't changed much since that first meeting. The face had been less masklike and the twitch of the lips more benign. But my first impressions were sidetracked by the state of his office. Even for a publisher, it was chaotic. Manuscripts and long sheets of galley proofs competed for space with books into which torn scraps of paper had been sandwiched to mark a place.

Framed photographs covered the walls. Most showed men in uniform, behind whom, in the middle distance, something smoked: a wrecked aircraft, a tank, a town. A common weary slouch conveyed wordlessly that they'd survived an ordeal. They eyed me warily, as if across a ravine that, however narrow, could never be traversed. It was the same look as on the faces of those young soldiers in the photographs displayed at the embassy. This is how fighting men always regard those who have not shared their experience. Though sometimes contemptuous, the look could also be kindly. *Be sorry you weren't here*, it seemed to say, *but be grateful too*.

Peter and I felt an instant rapport. For the rest of that first afternoon, we talked—or, rather, he talked and I listened. Too young for World War II and too old for Vietnam, he'd satisfied his taste for battlefield glory by becoming the most meticulous of military historians. A worldwide network of contacts gave him access to intelligence at the highest level. He could discourse on Erwin Rommel's admiration for von Clausewitz or the folly of Jeb Stuart at Gettysburg, then switch in a moment to an insider's view of the role of mercenaries in such African pestholes as Angola. Whatever the subject, however, his dryly ironic tone made war appear both the noblest of callings and the most futile.

As the light faded, he unlocked a drawer in his desk and took out a gun. With a lurch of the heart, I recognized that most glamorously menacing of automatic pistols, the Luger P08.

He checked the magazine and worked the action to satisfy himself it was unloaded, then held it out, butt first.

I took it in awe. I'd never before handled that chic, efficient implement of death.

"It's heavier than I expected," I said, weighing it.

"Good tools often are."

Reluctant to hand it back, I curled my hand around

The Luger P08 pistol

the butt. For the first time, the hunger it aroused in collectors became understandable to me.

Before I left, and almost as an afterthought, he agreed to publish my book. Maybe, he said, readers who liked stories about men being blown up would enjoy hearing about the men who blew them up, if only for the movies. But we both recognized that the reluctance with which I'd relinquished the Luger had tipped the scales. On some fundamental level, it revealed we were two of a kind.

When I returned a few weeks later to sign the contracts, however, Peter wasn't there.

"As it turns out, I'll be handling your book," said the editor who'd introduced us. "Just initial the bottom of each page."

"What about Mr. van Diemen?"

"Peter isn't . . . um . . . well, he won't be around for a while."

"Is he ill?"

"Not exactly . . ."

Over a plowman's lunch at the pub, the story emerged.

Peter lived with a particularly ill-tempered companion: wife or mistress, nobody knew exactly. But she often turned up at the office for visits that ended with embarrassingly loud arguments. The managing editor called Peter into his office for A Quiet Word, and the scenes ceased. The reason emerged a few weeks after Peter and I first met. Golfers on a remote suburban course found a corpse. Dissected, polyethylene-wrapped, and buried in a dense patch of rough, it might have remained undiscovered had inquisitive foxes not dug it up. Reassembled, the pieces were identified as Peter's lady friend.

Owning up without embarrassment to the police, Peter described her death as an accident: a wild punch at the culmination of yet another row. Since nobody had a good word to say about the victim, a sympathetic jury gave him the benefit of the doubt and five years for man-slaughter. He served three.

He wrote me a courteous note when the stuntman book was published, and after his release, we shared a lunch. How, I asked, was life outside prison?

"A bit lonely. I miss having a girlfriend, but I'm out of touch. It's difficult, finding women."

They had trouble finding your last one, I thought, but, diplomatic for once, said nothing.

13

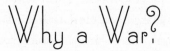

Why a War?

War is a series of catastrophes that results in a victory.
GEORGES CLEMENCEAU,
French prime minister

Every historian has a different explanation for World War I, but all agree that vanity, incompetence, and sheer bad timing all played a part.

By 1914, many politicians suspected that only a war could settle the festering feuds and clear the bad blood that troubled Europe.

Germany, whose sixteen states had united in 1871 under the most warlike of them, Prussia, was itching to prove itself. Flexing its military and industrial muscles, it stared around belligerently at the neighbors crowding its frontiers.

Staring back was France, still furious about the loss of Alsace.

Germans watched the maneuvers and exercises of France's military with as much alarm as they saw Britain expanding its fleet and Russia creating an enormous land army on its eastern border. Not unreasonably, Kaiser Wilhelm II believed these three nations, united by treaty, plotted to encircle Germany and limit its expansion, if not dismantle it entirely. Given the efficiency with which the British navy blockaded German ports in 1914, cutting off its imports, those fears were justified.

In anticipation, the German high command expanded its fleet and extended the national rail network. If war came, the planners in Berlin's Wilhelmstrasse wanted troops to arrive at the front in hours, not days, and fresh rather than exhausted by marching. Meanwhile, factories such as Krupp and I. G. Farben developed weapons of mass destruction: canisters of poison gas and guns so massive their shells arced briefly into space before plunging to earth at a speed faster than sound. These cannon could fire a projective forty miles. The maximum range of the French 75 mm was six.

The French might be excused for failing to foresee the power of long-range artillery, since it had never been an area of French expertise. In aviation, however, France led the world. Its pilots were the first to cross the English Channel and the Mediterranean, and while the Germans led in airship design, France pioneered fast-pursuit aircraft. It should have entered the war with a powerful air force. Instead, like the British, it struggled to catch up with Germany.

The aircraft and munitions factories of France and Britain didn't prepare for war because nobody really believed it would happen. For one thing, business would suffer. In July 1914, just a month before Europe mobilized, an American journalist lectured the French on its absurdity.

I have been waiting twenty-five years for your
European war. Many a time it has seemed as
imminent as this. But it will not come! Europe
cannot afford a war. There is today such a close
interrelationship between big business in the capitals
of Europe that an actual conflict is beyond the realm
of possibility. The diplomats will fume and fuss.
But they know better than to plunge their countries

into a colossal struggle that will ruin Europe and set
back civilization.

The very idea of war, along with its associated technologies, became the plaything of fantasy. Ever since the Franco-Prussian War, writers had speculated about the rise of a militant Germany. In 1871, British writer George Tomkyns Chesney published *The Battle of Dorking: Reminiscences of a Volunteer*, in which a thinly disguised Germany invaded and defeated Britain. Jules Verne dramatized submarine power in *20,000 Leagues Under the Sea* and H. G. Wells's 1907 *The War in the Air* foresaw Germany, joined by China and Japan, bombing the United States and Europe into ruin.

In France, however, both the public and intellectuals looked on military aviation as an amusing conceit. In the 1880s and 1890s, illustrator Albert Robida anticipated a war in which aircraft played a large part, but readers preferred his jokey suggestions about the French upper classes stepping into private airships rather than carriages. In his 1909 *Aeropolis*, Belgian Henry Kistemaeckers and French illustrator René Vincent imagined personal aircraft taking off from art nouveau balconies

Aeropolis. *Future aviation, as imagined in 1909 by René Vincent*

in the more fashionable arrondissements of Paris. At the end of *Aeropolis*, sinister Japanese arrive to menace Paris, but if anyone in Europe saw this as a warning, they took no notice.

War did come all the same, with shocking speed and largely by accident. On June 28, 1914, a group of young Serbian anarchists, incensed at Austria's annexation of their country, swore to kill Franz Ferdinand, Archduke of Austria, on a visit to the Bosnian town of Sarajevo. All suffered from tuberculosis, in those days incurable, and so felt they had nothing to lose.

Armed with bombs and handguns, and with cyanide suicide pills in their pockets, the six lined the motorcade route. Their efforts at assassination were inept. Most lost their nerve. One threw his bomb too late and blew up the car behind the archduke's. Then he swallowed his cyanide pill and jumped into the river, intending to drown. The water was only four inches deep and the pill was so old it just made him throw up.

At the end of the day, the last plotter, nineteen-year-old Gavrilo Princip, a melancholy idealist, stood eating a sandwich and brooding about the debacle. As the police had switched routes following the first bomb, he'd had no chance even to draw his Browning automatic pistol, let alone fire it.

At that moment, to his astonishment, the archduke's car, having taken a wrong turn, entered his street. Trying to back up, the driver stalled right in front of

Princip. Dropping his sandwich, he shoved through the crowd and, with two unlucky shots, fatally wounded both Franz Ferdinand and his wife. Blaming the Serbian government, Austria invaded, an act that automatically activated treaties committing France, Britain, and Russia to go to war with the Austro-Hungarian empire and its ally, Germany.

To fight over Serbia, an insignificant pawn in the international game, was ridiculous. But the killings took place in July. Military and political leaders were on holiday, and governments in recess. A power vacuum existed, and war rushed to fill it. Even then, Germany tried to put on the brakes. Between the kaiser, on holiday on a boat off Norway, and Czar Nicholas II in Saint Petersburg, cables bounced back and forth. In them, Willy urged cousin Nicky not to mobilize his army. Nicky, notoriously weak, stubborn, and not very bright, instead listened to his generals, stood on his dignity, and dithered. Nobody, it seems, knew how to *partially* mobilize Russia's enormous but unwieldy army. Finally, on July 31, Nicky wired, "It is technically impossible to stop our military preparations which were obligatory owing to Austria's mobilization."

As diplomacy failed, the German generals saw their chance and activated the Schlieffen plan, their best-kept military secret. Ignoring Belgium's neutrality and not waiting for the kaiser to sign an official declaration of war, they sent 1.4 million troops speeding there on the new railway system.

The tiny country on the North Sea became a back door through which they could enter France from the north, bypassing its forts. If, as they anticipated, France surrendered quickly, they planned to attack Russia before its army had assembled. As for Britain, Berlin regarded it as essentially a naval power and no threat on land. Taken completely by surprise, the French armies under General Joffre fell back on Paris. Even as printers were churning out postcards showing Alsatian women tearfully thanking French soldiers for liberating them, they were in full retreat. On September 7, they halted the Germans at the Marne, forty miles outside Paris. With minor variations, the two sides remained in stalemate until November 1918. Strategically, the war was over, at least in Europe. In terms of carnage, however, it had barely begun.

14

Archie Agonistes

There is indescribable enthusiasm and entire unanimity throughout Australia in support of all that tends to provide for the security of the empire in war.

SIR RONALD CRAUFURD MUNRO-FERGUSON,
governor-general of Australia, in a message to the
colonial secretary in London, July 1914

*W*hy would Australians agree to fight in a war on the far side of the world?

They didn't. They were never asked. As one historian explained:

Australia didn't even have to declare war. Britain, as head of the family, spoke on behalf of her empire. All Australia had to decide was the

extent of its participation. Most Australians saw
nothing unusual in this. They also saw themselves
as Britons, far from home, it was true, and in a
strange land where the trees shed their bark instead
of their leaves, but they were still Britons and wore
three-piece suits in the pitiless sun to prove it.

No Australian was forced to enlist, least of all my grandfather. Even had the draft existed, he could have claimed exemption as a family man. But he volunteered anyway. Nobody knows his reasons at first hand, since just as our family never talked to one another, they also seldom wrote letters or kept diaries. Once you know the Baxter character, however, some pieces of evidence speak more loudly than any words.

One is another early photograph of Archie. It was taken on his wedding day in 1906. Clutching a pair of white gloves in one hand, he is a picture of exquisite discomfort in his first formal suit. He's irresistibly reminiscent of the barrow boy hero in the popular dialect poem of C. J. Dennis, *The Sentimental Bloke*, suffering through afternoon tea with the family of his middle-class sweetheart, Doreen.

Wedding photograph of Archie and Stella, 1906

Me cuffs kep' playin' wiv me nervis fears
Me patent leathers nearly brought the tears
An' there I sits wiv "Yes, mum. Thanks. Indeed?"
Me stand-up collar sorin' orf me ears.

Archie's other arm is linked with that of Stella
Madden, his Doreen. Her steel-rimmed spectacles and
prim mouth suggest the same inflexible disposition as
the mother in Dennis's poem. Cousins and friends flank
them, but the eye is drawn to a truculent gent with a

bushy mustache, seated to one side. He's John Madden, father of the bride.

*B*oth Madden and his daughter exhibit the same no-nonsense mouth, the unflinching gaze. In contrast, Archie, big-eared, wide-eyed, trusting, looks as rural as the town where he was born. Burrawang, in dense bushland eighty miles from Sydney, is the classic mountain village. Anyone raised in the Ozarks or the Blue Ridge, on a Swiss hillside, or in the forests of the Auvergne would instantly be at home among its thick-walled houses of local sandstone, their roofs steeply pitched to shed snow. There was even a local version of the troll, that monster of the European forests imported by emigrants to scare the children. The Burrawang bunyip lurked in a swamp, killing cattle by night but disappearing the moment anyone set out to catch it.

Bunyips notwithstanding, my great-grandfather James Baxter, a Scot from around Aberdeen, liked Burrawang and did well there. Back in Scotland, a branch of the Baxter family operated a lucrative business producing high-end canned goods: grouse, pheasant, poacher's broth, and haggis soup. Encouraged, James started a bacon factory. It flourished, but it also helped kill him. His obituary in the local paper, *The Scrutineer* of August 28, 1891, described how "some twelve month ago he began to feel the effects of constant and undue pressure upon his stomach leaning over the edge of the bacon curing vats."

James fathered nine daughters and three sons. On his death, the bacon factory and his two-hundred-acre farm with ninety cattle and six horses went to his widow, Eliza, and, after she died, to his eldest, Archie. He liquidated his father's property and moved to Sydney.

With the profits of the sale in his pocket, Archie was a catch. And caught he was, by the Madden family, in the person of Margaret Stella Isabella Madden, always known as Stella. Continuing our family's involvement with food, Archie took a job as a "canvasser," or traveling salesman, in his case for groceries, and bought a spacious house in the inner-city suburb of Leichhardt. The couple moved in. So, however, did Stella's father, and her brother, Claude.

Few recipes for disaster are more poisonous than living with one's in-laws. (I could only nod in agreement at the line in the film *Field of Dreams*: "We lived with my wife's parents as long as we could, almost an entire afternoon.") There's a certain irony, as well as a sense of the inevitability that runs through our family, that, as children, we should have shared the same house with our in-laws, and soon been at one another's throats.

Did Archie feel himself caught in the same trap? Historian Peter Stanley, analyzing the makeup of the first volunteers to the AIF, cites "evading domestic responsibilities" as a significant motive for wanting to leave the country. Whatever his reasons, Archie appears to have needed little urging to abandon his family and, in particular, Stella's, to fight someone else's battles on the far side of the world. As Pasternak says in *Doctor Zhivago*, "Happy men don't volunteer."

❋ · 15 · ❋

The Call to Arms

We don't want to fight, but by Jingo if we do
We've got the ships, we've got the men, we've got the
money too.

E. H. MCDERMOTT

But why would he do that?" Marie-Dominique asked.

"Maybe Archie just wanted to escape."

She looked doubtful. "You would never leave us to go and fight in Australia—would you?"

I knew enough of France and married life not to answer that question.

Convinced of France's superiority to all other countries, the French don't understand why anyone would want to leave, even to fight on its behalf. Rather than send Frenchmen to defend their colonies in Asia and

Africa, they farmed out the job. The Légion Etrangère, the French Foreign Legion, accepted, indeed invited, the world's toughest nuts. You could enlist under whatever name you chose. Nobody asked about your reasons. The Foreign Legion, in the words of one writer, "developed into a collective exercise in convenient amnesia, acquiring a reputation as a haven for cut-throats, crooks and sundry fugitives from justice. Few questions were put to new recruits, making it an ideal repository for the scum of the earth. And with the scum came the romantics, men searching for a way to dull the pain of doomed love."

Doomed love? Might that be why Archie left? Was there another woman? I wouldn't have been surprised. Abrupt marriages, divorces, and quixotic romantic gestures pepper our family history. Two aunts married American servicemen during World War II. Both returned soon after, each with a child. My own father wasn't married to my mother when I was born. For good measure, he had been married before. That I was fifty years old before he told me says something about the Baxters' chronic inability to communicate.

Or had Archie simply felt the same nationalist euphoria as Britain? Britons needed no more excuse to join up than the ground beneath their feet. When Eleanor

Farjeon asked the poet Edward Thomas why he chose to enlist, he stooped, scooped up a handful of earth, and said, "Literally, for this." Many in Britain accepted the propaganda maps, supposedly discovered by British spies, showing how postwar Europe would look if the Germans won: a *Gross-Deutschland* extending from Saint Petersburg to the Spanish border, with the British Isles as a *Deutsche-Kolonie*. Britain a colony of Germany? Unthinkable.

Even without any mystical love of the soil, one could imagine Australians responding to a similar nationalism. Australia had only existed as a nation since its six states federated in 1901, which made it barely older than the united Germany. One couldn't fight for one's country if one didn't have a country, but now that they did, both Aussies and Germans found patriotism a novel and exciting concept.

I tried to imagine Archie metaphorically wrapped in the flag of the Southern Cross. It wasn't easy. He didn't seem the type. But what *was* the type?

The "digger" image of the Great War was largely the creation of a single artist, Norman Lindsay. He was one of those belligerent little men whom Australia finds both admirable and exasperating. Billy Hughes, the wartime prime minister, was another, compensating for poor health and short stature with a furious output of work. Historian Les Carlyon described Hughes as "cranky and deaf and dyspeptic, but still bustling with energy, cracking out abuse to his hapless typists, carried along by the fever of war."

Though Lindsay was less than half Hughes's age, he had the same arrogance. Bigotry came naturally to him. Fanatically nationalist, he was also anti-Semitic, anti-Black, anti-gay—probably anti-Eskimo too, had anyone thought to ask. Though almost the same age as Pablo Picasso and James Joyce, he loathed the work of both and detested anything in art or literature that smelled of modernism—a prejudice he shared with Kaiser Wilhelm, who feared the new in everything but instruments of war.

Lindsay's style, rooted in nineteenth-century French history painting, ran mostly to female nudes with Amazonian breasts and wrestlers' thighs. When, however, in 1914 the popular weekly *The Bulletin* asked for anti-German cartoons, he leaped to the drawing board to create the archetypal Hun. A drooling beast, half-naked, always in the pointed helmet known as a *pickelhaube*, these monsters rampaged through his drawings,

*Norman Lindsay.
Monsters of Depravity
and Children of Light.*

raping buxom Belgians and trampling babies underfoot. For good measure they sometimes carried a hatchet or meat cleaver, dripping blood.

At the same time, he created the archetypal Aussie: clean-cut, sturdy, muscular, white, a model of Aryan supremacy in skin-tight khaki shirt, riding boots, jodhpurs, and a slouch hat—the very antithesis of the real digger, often slouching, untidy, and belligerent. Art historian Bernard Smith acknowledged that Lindsay's war cartoons "invariably presented Germans as monsters of depravity, the Allies as the children of light." The propagandizing was almost too flagrant. During World War II, when it seemed the Nazis and Japanese might overwhelm even Australia, his wife, fearing Germans with long memories, urged him to flee to America.

Might Archie have been moved by such crude flag-waving? It wasn't so great a stretch, since I admired Lindsay myself, for his technique rather than his subject matter, and owned some of his less bellicose work. He lived in the same mountains outside Sydney as my parents, and I often drove down the bush lane that ran past his house, slowing to read the sign NO PAINTINGS FOR SALE on the gate. After his death, his house became a museum. We could inspect at leisure his spacious canvases and stroll in his garden, dotted with life-sized sculptures of husky nudes, incongruously molded in gray cement.

I was still puzzling over Archie's possible motives when another old friend came to the rescue.

I met Michael when we were asked by one of the

cinema bureaucracies to distribute funds to makers of Australian short films. During a week of interviews with greedy, argumentative, and only occasionally gifted applicants, we'd come to feel like soldiers trapped in a shell hole during an artillery barrage.

Michael became a military historian and producer of films about Australia's war effort. When he passed through France, I shamelessly picked his brain.

"When did your grandfather enlist?"

"May 1916."

"Hmmm. That was a low point. We'd lost twenty-eight thousand at Ypres and just as many at Gallipoli, but the British were pushing for more men."

Prime Minister Hughes wanted conscription, but only if voters approved: many Australians still resented the governor-general's automatic assumption in 1914 that they would fight with Britain. Twice Hughes took the question to the country in a plebiscite; twice it was rejected. Even troops on the front line in France, who stood to benefit most from reinforcements, refused to support compulsory military service. "I wouldn't wish this place on my worst enemy," said one.

"What surprises me," I said, "is the fact that Archie enlisted even though he had a wife and child. Who was supposed to look after them?"

"Australian soldiers got very good pay. Some of his would have gone to his wife. Enough to live on. And the recruiters wouldn't have discouraged him. They took pretty well anyone."

Michael explained the new tools now available to the researcher into Australia's military history. Almost as much as the French, the Australians, it seemed, had embraced their *patrimoine*, particularly if it carried a rifle.

"Just go into the site of the Australian War Memorial or the National Archives and put in his name. Everything that ever happened to an Australian serviceman is cataloged five different ways." He smiled. "Even the lice have serial numbers."

"Would it show whether he experienced anything remarkable in France?"

"Remarkable? You mean more remarkable than being shot, bayoneted, blown up, gassed?"

"Something more personal. Intimate." I explained about the *cité des ténèbres* and *San Fairy Ann*.

"Well, some weird stuff did go on," he said. "When I get back, I'll send you some books. There's been an enormous amount published about things that previously got swept under the carpet."

"You mean desertions? Executions at dawn? That sort of thing?"

Real Australian diggers at a camp in Wiltshire, 1917

"Oh, yes, all those. But I was thinking of the mutinies, rapes, murders. And the mystical stuff too: miraculous interventions, angels . . ."

He looked at the gray sky that seemed to be settling on the metal roofs of the city as if to stifle us.

"It's something to do with France. War here was . . ." Shaking his head as if to dislodge a troubling thought, he turned up his collar. "You think it's going to rain?"

I watched him disappear down the winding staircase of our apartment building. *Murders. Rapes. Angels?* Clearly I had a lot to learn.

· 16 ·

They Knew

*Is there any hope that it will not be war? If Austria at-
tacks Serbia, why should that mean that France must
attack Germany and my boys go to be killed? Serbia is
nothing but a name to me. And yet I must suffer this.
Tell me, is such a thing possible?*

ANONYMOUS FRENCH MOTHER IN AUGUST 1914,
reported by Herbert Adams Gibbons

The sage-green boxes of the booksellers known as
bouquinistes line both banks of the Seine from the
Musée d'Orsay to Notre Dame. They are as much a
tourist attraction as the caricaturists of Montmartre's
Place du Tertre and the accordion virtuosi who work
the métro along line 1, La Défense–Château de Vin-
cennes, reminding us that man's ingenuity can always
find new ways to mangle "La Vie en Rose."

But just as no Parisian ever poses for a caricature or encourages the buskers by giving them money, only tourists buy from the *bouquinistes*. Not only are their books overpriced; most are tightly wrapped in cellophane and Scotch tape. Try to discover if one has all its pages or somebody has used a slice of *jambon sec* as a bookmark and the seller will come bolting from his stool at the sunny edge of the sidewalk to snatch it from your fumbling fingers.

But travel any weekend to the fifteenth arrondissement, on the southern edge of the city, and you find a different atmosphere. Only the trade knows the year-round market for old books at the Espace George Brassens. They call it colloquially by the name of the street on which it stands, rue Brancion.

It's at Brancion that the treasures surface, hauled in from the country by jobbers who've cleared the stock of a bankrupt bookshop or the shelves of a country house. Ignoring the professionals who range leather-bound rarities alphabetically on custom-built collapsible shelves, these shifty characters pile their loot on trestle tables at one euro each, or five books for three, and watch clients descend like vultures on fresh kill.

The high-gabled open-sided pavilions with their stone-flagged floors were once an equine slaughterhouse. A bronze horse head over the gate reminds us of the animals that died here, as does the statue of an aproned *fort*, or strongman, with a side of beef draped as casually over his shoulders as a 1920s matron's fur tippet.

Why had Peter van Diemen suggested we meet here? Probably because he knew that on weekends, particularly when the weather was warm, I could often be found browsing the tables piled with books, magazines, maps, and ephemera.

A bigger question was, why did he want to meet at all? His call, like everything else about him, was unexpected. Had we exchanged phone numbers? I didn't remember giving him mine. And we're not listed in the phone book.

"Our chat at the embassy got me thinking," he had said on the phone. "I believe I could help you with your project."

There was no "project." And I wasn't sure I wanted Peter van Diemen in my life. But to someone who had, after all, killed a woman with his bare hands, attention had to be paid.

"That's great," I said, with an enthusiasm I didn't feel. "When are you free?"

I spotted him before he saw me, and I stood for a

moment, letting the damp and cold of the stone flags seep through the soles of my shoes.

T. S. Eliot wrote of his hollow men having "shape without form, shade without colour." That was Peter. His gabardine overcoat, the indeterminate hue of cigarette ash, could have been made in the 1920s and hung at the back of a closet ever since, sagging into shapelessness as all color leached into the dark. His brown lace-up shoes, thick-soled, scuffed but well kept, belonged to another era as well, when footwear was made by hand, kept stretched on shoe trees between wearings, and, at country-house weekends, placed outside the guest's door to be polished overnight by the boot boy.

His dress and manner made him as insubstantial and diaphanous as a background extra in a black-and-white movie. In the week following the murder, he made five return trips by bus to the golf course where he buried the body, each time carrying dismembered portions in a large suitcase. And yet the police, interviewing bus drivers and people who traveled regularly on the same line, could find no one who remembered him.

> *Yesterday, upon the stair*
> *I met a man who wasn't there . . .*

As if the thought signaled my presence, he turned and saw me. His smile was less thin today, almost warm. Or was I just getting used to it?

"So you found me."

I nodded at the stock of the dealer beside whose stand we'd met. "It wasn't too hard."

Not all sellers at Brancion specialized, but I knew that the middle-aged woman who sat impassively on a hard chair, ignoring us as she smoked a Gauloise and leafed through *Aladdin*, the monthly magazine for *chineurs*—antiques people—sold only militaria.

"Adele often has interesting things. Like this."

He unrolled a yellowing sheet of paper, placing books at the corners to keep it flat. The uncompromising Didot roman typeface proclaimed it as a French government notice, designed to be read even by people to whom reading did not come naturally.

> *ARMY OF LAND AND ARMY OF SEA.*
> *ORDER OF GENERAL MOBILIZATION*
> *By decree of the President of the Republic, the*
> *mobilization of the armies of land and sea is*
> *ordered, as well as the requisition of animals,*
> *carriages and harness necessary to the supplying*
> *of these armies.*

THE FIRST DAY OF
THE MOBILIZATION IS
Sunday, August 3, 1914
Every Frenchman, subject to military obligation,
must, under penalty of being punished with all the
rigor of the law, obey the prescriptions of his book of
mobilization.

Subject to this order are ALL MEN not at
present under the flag.

The civil and military Authorities are responsible
for the execution of this decree.
THE MINISTER OF WAR,
THE MINISTER OF THE NAVY.

"It's original?" I asked.

"Oh, yes. These aren't particularly rare. A copy
would have been posted in every town hall, every police
station, every railway station and post office—and not
only in continental France but Corsica, Algeria, and all
the French dependencies as well. That's what makes this
so fascinating."

My incomprehension showed. But fortunately obses-
sives love to explain.

"For this poster to be available in all those places on

the same day, *it had to be printed and distributed in advance.*"

His finger stabbed at the date of mobilization. It wasn't printed like the rest but stamped by hand.

I could visualize the policemen, customs officers, or postmasters putting down the phone and leaving their lunch to hurry to the office. They'd have rummaged in their stationery cupboard for the poster sent days—even weeks?—before, with orders to hold it until . . . well, until a German platoon on maneuvers took a wrong turn and crossed a frontier or some drunk sentry at an Alsatian border post fired at his opposite number on the other side. Or a dying boy in an obscure Croatian town put a couple of bullets into a midlevel Austrian aristo and his lady.

Taking the stamp with which they dated all correspondence, the officials would have breathed on it to moisten the ink and inserted in the blank space the precise moment on which the world went to war.

"They knew," said Peter quietly. "Weeks, even months before. They *knew*."

All the way back from Brancion, an obscure fact nibbled at my memory. The source came to me just as I arrived home. From my shelves, the vivid orange cloth and art deco spine of Nina Hamnett's memoir *Laughing Torso* almost leaped out. Sculptor, model, friend of Modigliani, and, in her day, lover of almost everyone else in Montparnasse, Hamnett had been in Paris in 1914. Her lover at the time, a German, was briefly interned at the Prefecture. Few Germans were. "He had known many Germans as we all did," she wrote. "Oddly enough, a few days before the declaration of war, all the Germans vanished from the Quarter."

If the French knew what was coming, it seemed the Germans did as well.

✳ · 17 · ✳

But We Think You Ought to Go

We've watched you playing cricket and every kind of game,
At football, golf and polo you men have made your name.
But now your country calls you to play your part in war.
And no matter what befalls you
We shall love you all the more.
So come and join the forces
As your fathers did before.

PAUL RUBENS,

lyrics to "Your King and Country Want You," 1914

The Paris métro line 4, Porte de Clignancourt–Porte d'Orléans, runs right by the foot of our street, rue de l'Odéon. A few days after meeting Peter at Brancion, I took it northbound. At the Château d'Eau stop, I surfaced onto boulevard de Strasbourg, into a cluster of grinning young Africans offering suspect mobile phone cards.

A few blocks away, the façade of the Gare de l'Est, the eastern station, marked the end of the boulevard. It hadn't changed much since 1914. Back then, even the phone card vendors would have had their contemporary equivalents—*voyous* selling tip sheets with guaranteed winners at Chantilly and Longchamp, or copies of the sports papers that handicapped the bike races at the Vél d'Hiv.

From the moment of mobilization, attention in France shifted to the railways. With little public road transport and almost no private cars, they were the commonest form of travel. On that Sunday in August 1914, the morning of mobilization, passengers on expresses heading into Paris found their carriages invaded. "We were besieged by crowds of reservists," an American wrote, "until there was no more room and the engine could draw no more extra carriages. Then we crept slowly toward Paris, bearing our offering of human lives. One could feel, mingled with the effervescence, the excitement, the joy of approaching conflict, an undertone of anguish and sorrow."

A French journalist felt differently.

At every station, reservists got on. Workers and peasants mostly, with their poor baggage. They clogged the corridors, because there were already fifteen people in every compartment meant for ten. As more boarded at Maintenon, Chartres and Nogent, they moved into the first class; these brave men among officers; respectful, disciplined, confident. They spoke among themselves and very intelligently with us about the different phases of the crisis. All of them read the papers regularly. They understood perfectly the true character of the crisis. One said, "It had to happen. We've been insulted for forty-four years." Another said, "We aren't sad. We're serious." It was true. They didn't sing. They didn't demonstrate. They embodied, these humble men, the firm dignity of the nation.

Arriving in Paris at one of the *grandes gares*, the great railway stations, conscripts had to make their way to the designated rallying point for their unit, usually a large café. From there, they were sent to an embarkation point. For most, that was the Gare de l'Est. Many found it easier to walk. From a restaurant in the rue Royale, Edith Wharton watched them pass.

The street was flooded by the torrent of people. All were on foot, and carrying their luggage; for since dawn every cab and taxi and motor-omnibus had disappeared. The crowd that passed our window was chiefly composed of conscripts who were on the way to the station. Wives and families trudged beside them, carrying all kinds of odd improvised bags and bundles. The faces ceaselessly streaming by were serious but not sad; nor was there any air of bewilderment—the stare of driven cattle. All these lads and young men seemed to know what they were about and why they were about it. The youngest of them looked suddenly grown up and responsible; they understood their stake in the job, and accepted it.

Contingents from other nations marched with them. They carried hastily prepared banners assuring their support.

Rumania Rallies to the Mother of the Latin Races
Italy, Whose Freedom Was Purchased with French
  Blood
Spain, the Loving Sister of France

Greeks Who Love France
Scandinavians of Paris
South American Lives for the Mother of South
*   American Culture*

Loud cheers greeted BELGIUM LOOKS TO FRANCE and LUXEMBOURG WILL NEVER BE GERMAN, but the crowd really went wild as a group passed under the banner AL-SATIANS GOING HOME.

Summer holidays in France always begin on August 1. It's an immovable feast, as cut in stone as Christmas Day or France's national day, July 14. In any other August, Parisians would have been streaming out of the city, heading for that almost mystical reunion with the region of their birth that is central to the French *vacances*.

Their numbers would have been swelled by foreign tourists, many headed for the Gare de l'Est to board the Orient Express, traveling via Strasbourg, Munich, Vienna, Budapest, and Bucharest to Istanbul. Normally these well-heeled travelers crowded the departure hall, exchanging kisses and going-away gifts as porters hus-

Gare de l'Est, August 1914

tled brass-bound trunks into the luggage vans.

Instead, this August, to their astonishment, most were sent home. Only military trains were running. A cartoon showed a man telling a railway man, "I'm in a hurry. I've got to be somewhere in two hours," and the official replying, "Alsace has been waiting for 44 years. You're not saying your impatience compares with hers?" Edith Wharton, who had no travel plans, took perverse satisfaction in the tourists' comeuppance. "The civilians who had not bribed and jammed their way into a cranny of the thronged carriages leaving the first night could only creep back through the hot streets to their hotel and wait. Back they went, to the resounding emptiness of porterless halls, waiterless restaurants, motionless lifts: to the queer disjointed life of fashionable hotels suddenly reduced to the intimacies and makeshift of a Latin Quarter *pension*."

For the young reservists, being in Paris on their way to war was better than a holiday. Tanned farm boys, seeing a city for the first time, gaped at the cars, the crowds, the vaulted ceiling of the Gare de l'Est. In the patois of Brittany and Normandy, they drawled their astonishment to uncomprehending street kids, pale and rat-thin, freshly rousted by the police from the lanes of Montmartre. Over the next few years, deaths at the front would confer on this terminus a sinister, even menacing, character. When someone asked after an absent son, father, or husband, women would say somberly, "He was eaten by the East."

Today, I had no trouble crossing the wide courtyard in front of the station, but in August 1914 it would have been a struggle. Conscripts and their families blocked the area solid, joined by the curious and the frustrated private passengers. Residents around the square looked down on an ocean of straw hats, the traditional summer headgear of the average Parisian,

either the stiff *canotiers* the British called "boaters," or soft Panamas, so popular that the slang term for Paris's working-class suburbs was "Panama," shortened to "Panam."

Many in the crowd that day were drunk, either from elation or despair. When a café opposite the station tried to exploit this by raising prices, customers rampaged through its three floors, smashing every piece of glass. English and American journalists who came to investigate were boosted onto tabletops and ordered, in celebration of the Triple Alliance, to sing "My Country 'Tis of Thee" and "God Save the Queen."

Le Départ des Poilus, Août
1914 *by Albert Herter*

Fortunately, the architects who renovated the Gare
de l'Est in 1931 preserved its windowed stone halls.
Hanging overhead in one of them was the painting I'd
come to see. *Le Départ des Poilus, Août 1914* is eighty
meters square—almost as wide and tall as the railway
carriage it depicts. The American artist Albert Herter
painted it in 1926 and presented it to the nation. Since
then, it's been on display here, first along the wall of the
departure hall, then higher up, where one can admire
the composition, even if the details aren't so clear.

It shows a typical scene of August 1914. Fathers in
uniform say good-bye to their families. Husbands hug

wives. One man, apparently in despair, sits with his head in his hands. Young men crowd the carriage windows, most in shirtsleeves because of the heat. A few look excited. Others are indifferent. At the center of the composition, one boy stands in a doorway, kepi in one hand, carbine in the other, arms flung out in a gesture that could represent either ecstasy or protest. The lily jutting from the barrel of his rifle is ambiguous; is it there as the symbol of Bourbon France or as the traditional Anglo-Saxon flower of funerals? No less enigmatic are the figures of a gray-bearded man on the far right and a woman with clasped hands on the left. Neither looks at the soldiers. The man carries a bunch of flowers and has laid his hand on his heart. The woman looks pensively into the middle distance, her mind elsewhere.

The canvas trades in that sense of time lost and regained that preoccupied Proust and Cocteau. For Herter, as for many writers and artists who found their material in the war, mixing the present and the past became a form of denial, a refusal to accept the waste and anarchy.

The older couple are Herter and his wife. The exultant boy is Everit, their son, who would die in the war. Herter shows himself and his wife as they appeared in 1926, when he painted the picture, but Everit is as they last saw him, forever young.

As the Herters mourned their son, the British poet Laurence Binyon stood on Pentire Head in Cornwall, looking toward France. Thoughts of the dead inspired the poem he called "For the Fallen." It became so treasured that a plaque on the spot celebrates the moment.

In the poem, Binyon suggests that war has made the casualties immortal.

They shall grow not old, as we that are left grow old:
Age shall not weary them, nor the years condemn.
At the going down of the sun, and in the morning
We will remember them.

By showing the loss of loved ones in a more optimistic light, "For the Fallen" comforted the bereaved. It became an anthem, and remains one. In Returned Soldiers League clubs across Australia, at 9:00 p.m. every night, the rattle and crash of the poker machines ceases. At the bar, glasses are lowered and hands laid on hearts. As the lights dim, curtains part on a tabernacle in which burns an eternal, albeit electric, flame. A recorded voice recites the verse beginning "They shall grow not old," at the end of which everyone mumbles "Lest we forget."

Nobody remembers the poem's other lines, which propose an even sunnier upside to the war.

Death august and royal
Sings sorrow up into immortal spheres.
There is music in the midst of desolation
And a glory that shines upon our tears.

Such sentimentality angered Wilfred Owen, who might have had Binyon in his sights when, in 1917, he evoked a gas attack and its horrible casualties. Remembering the words from the Roman poet Horace chiseled into the wall of the chapel at Sandhurst, the military academy—DULCE ET DECORUM EST PRO PATRIA MORI: it is sweet and fitting to die for one's country—Owen lashed out at those who traded in spurious glory or clung to it for reassurance.

If you could hear, at every jolt, the blood
Come gargling from the froth-corrupted lungs,
Obscene as cancer, bitter as the cud
Of vile, incurable sores on innocent tongues,
My friend, you would not tell with such high zest
To children ardent for some desperate glory,
The old Lie: Dulce et decorum est
Pro patria mori.

· 18 ·

The War to End Wars Inc.

The chief business of the American people is business.
They are profoundly concerned with producing, buying,
selling, investing and prospering in the world. I am
strongly of the opinion that the great majority of people
will always find these are moving impulses of our life.

CALVIN COOLIDGE,

thirtieth president of the United States

The journalist who warned that war would be bad for business was speaking of Europe, not the United States. In 1914, American arms and munitions manufacturers in particular rubbed their hands, since the Allies, unable to match the output of German factories, would be forced to buy from them.

As Britain and France liquidated their U.S. holdings to foot these bills, New York's investment houses were quick to extend credit—at the usual rates. By June 1915, France was so desperate for hard currency that it asked citizens to sell their gold to the Banque de France. This went against every instinct of a frugal, essentially peasant society, which had learned by experience that, in hard times, your best friends were a few gold *louis* buried under the hearthstone or hidden in an old shoe. Nevertheless, a trickle of patriotic citizens climbed the steps of the Banque de France to trade their jewelry and hoarded coins for paper money, a painful sacrifice, and finally in vain. By the end of the war, France and Germany were bankrupt and Britain deeply in debt.

The first businesses to be affected by the war were Paris's shops and cafés As the Germans advanced in early September 1914, thousands fled. For a few days, it seemed the city's population of about 1.5 million was reduced almost to nothing. "Paris deprived of its men of fighting age," one observer moaned. "Paris deserted by its fugitives. Paris silent and meditative. . . . Paris isn't Paris."

But the city was not so easily subdued. Those who remained, dismissing the runaways as *froussards*—panic merchants—turned out to be right. Once the front stabilized, cafés, cabarets, shops, and brothels reopened to brisk business as soldiers were rotated home on leave and Paris swelled with the bureaucracy of war. The returning runaways tried to put a defiant face on their flight. Cocteau wrote, "They all found an apology to offer for their departure. Some used their service as an excuse, others their little girl, their old mother, or their own person, too important to be taken hostage by the Germans. Others pleaded their Duty to The Nation."

Those who'd gone to England claimed they'd come back because they couldn't stand the food. Others who'd hidden with relatives at the far end of the country relied on bluster. One of them, taking his usual place in the café, began by announcing "Mark my words. We'll be in Berlin by Christmas." Looking up from his paper, a neighbor who hadn't fled asked innocently. "Oh, is that what they're saying *in Bordeaux*?"

This "business as usual" stance was the first sign that no matter how catastrophic the war news, life in the capital would continue with as little disturbance as possible. The Germans might have hung onto Alsace: they would not have Paris.

Now that the invaders were bogged down in their trenches, they didn't look so threatening. They were soon being mocked everywhere. The proximity of the

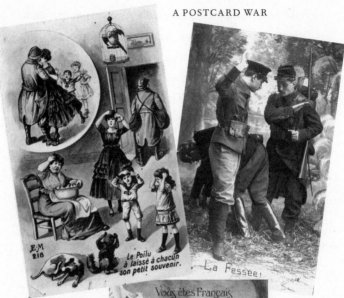

Poilus *on leave give everyone a gift—lice.*

Tommy and poilu spank the kaiser.

Alsatians thank Joffre.

front to a city full of artists and writers made this war the most comprehensively recorded in history. No conflict ever produced such an avalanche of fiction, poetry, music, photography, painting, and film. As long as everyone believed the war would be over by Christmas, there was a rush to document its triumphant progress. Once they saw otherwise, to stop would have been an admission of defeat.

Producers of postcards had never been so busy. For soldiers separated from their families for the first time, cards offered a form of communication that didn't require a high level of literacy. The forces also favored them, since they were easier to handle than letters, particularly for officers who were required to read and censor all mail. Armies on both sides printed their own lettercards that required no writing at all. They simply listed various alternatives—"I am well [ ], injured [ ], recovering [ ], a prisoner [ ] "—and the sender ticked the relevant box. More sophisticated correspondents sent cards with embroidered inserts or picture cards produced in series of eight. By exchanging these one at a time, a couple could conduct a courtship, leaving it to be consummated during the next leave.

In an inspired decision, the publishers of *L'Illustration* decided to devote its pages entirely to news of the war and its most glamorous personalities. From a prewar weekly circulation of 80,000, it leaped to 400,000 and maintained it until the armistice in 1918. Cheaper weeklies such as *Le Miroir* used less glossy paper and poorer reproduction to cover the same ground. Other publishers joined the rush with magazines featuring suggestive cartoons, pinups, caricatures, and war-related gossip. *Le Régiment* was aimed at officers on leave, in contrast to the more working-class *La Baïonnette*. Most influential of all, the glossy *La Vie Parisienne* filled its pages with drawings of half-nude girls, sexy but sharp-edged cartoons, and pages of small ads for erotic books and photographs and the services of *masseuses* and *manucuristes*.

The French, British, and Commonwealth armies all authorized artists to paint, photograph, and film life at the front. Initially, they documented the propagandists' claim that Germans had raped, murdered, and mutilated their way across what was generally called "Brave Little Belgium." The August 1914 issue of *L'Illustration* ran a full-page drawing of a German officer posed proudly in front of burning buildings with his foot on the body of a dead woman, the corpse of a baby lying just behind him to one side and that of a priest on the other.

However, as the horror stories were discredited, cartoonists lightened up. The *pickelhaube* became an object of derision rather than menace. Speculating on what might happen once the Germans began influencing their new allies, the Turks, a cartoonist showed the citizens of Constantinople forced to goose-step around the city, top their fezes with a spike, and squeeze the humps of their camels to a point.

Artists developed shorthand depictions of the leading players. The British were John Bull, the Americans Uncle Sam or the Statue of Liberty, France the stylized female figure Marianne, wearing the Phrygian cap adopted by the revolutionaries of 1789 as a symbol of freedom.

The Germans posed a problem, since different nations saw them in different ways. British, American, and Australian artists evoked the barbarians that overran Europe in the third century—the Huns. An archetype of the German emerged as a twentieth-century Hun—half man, half beast, sometimes naked but mostly in baggy trousers and boots, occasionally carrying a bloody ax but invariably wearing a *pickelhaube*. Norman Lindsay in particular drew these monsters with a pen that dripped race hatred and xenophobia.

To the French, Germans were less menacing—shambling gray creatures, dead-eyed, dumb as the vegetables after which they named them: turnips, potatoes or *krauts* and *boche*—cabbages. As an all-purpose insult, however, "Hun" won out. The U.S. forces newspaper *Stars and Stripes* reported, "It was too hard to get the proper pronunciation of 'boches.' The doughboys tried it with a long 'o' and with a short 'o.' Then they gave up. 'Get one of them Bushes for yourself and two for me' shouted a doughboy who had been left behind to a comrade departing for the trenches."

Under the camouflage of humor, satire magazines could snipe at the war and its commanders, unlike the daily press, forced to feed its readers propagandist drivel. The communiqués issued by the ministry of information each day at 3:00 p.m., while eagerly awaited, were seldom accurate and often bordered on fiction. Copies of Swiss papers were furiously sought as the only reliable source of war news. Censorship suppressed, for example, all reporting of the Taxis of the Marne, for fear it would reveal how comprehensively Joffre had been outmaneuvered. The most *L'Illustration* could do was tip a wink to the rumor mill by running a photograph of the empty parking area in front of the Gare de l'Est and commenting that taxis had been scarce for a few days.

The worse the reality of the front, the more jolly the terms in which the papers were forced to report it. During the disastrous 1915 spring offensive, a journalist wrote of the troops, "They are all light-hearted!

They are having fun!" If you believed the papers, the front resembled a holiday camp where *poilus* spent their days furnishing and decorating their dugouts like country cottages and painting signs that identified certain trenches as "Avenue Albert 1st" and "Boulevard Joffre."

Le Matin claimed the trenches had produced a new species of individual, called, in untranslatable slang, a *fourbancier*. This prodigy was "a colourful character, a jack of all trades, a born handyman, an inventor. He's a Robinson Crusoe without a Friday, for whom it's always Sunday. He can knock up the bed head, the candle stick *and* the candle." In startlingly bad taste, the report evoked the 1816 wreck of the ship *Medusa*. Of 147 people who piled onto a raft, only 15 survived, after eating one another. "On the raft of the *Medusa*," joked the journalist, a *fourbancier* "would have unearthed some green peas and knocked up a delicious stew from old boots."

This picture of industrious craftwork and inspired scrounging wasn't entirely without foundation. Every unit on both sides had a few such individuals. The platoon in Erich Maria Remarque's *All Quiet on the Western Front* has "Kat" Katczinsky, who "can find anything—camp stoves and firewood when it is cold, hay and straw, tables, chairs—but above all he can find food. No one understands how he does it, and it's as if he conjures it out of

All Quiet on the Western Front. *The fantasy of trench warfare—pets and a little light gardening*

thin air. His masterpiece was four cans of lobster. (Mind you, we would really have preferred dripping instead.)"

Common soldiers with handicraft skills, no matter what their nationality, made good use of the scrap metal, wood, wire, and glass littering the battlefield. "Trench art" crafted by bored but handy troops included badges and money clips, brass matchboxes, and cigarette lighters made from cartridge cases. The casing from a 75 mm cannon shell lent itself to embossing or engraving and was just the right size for a flower vase. Such items became a form of currency, exchanged among the troops and occasionally with the enemy. Though trench art was produced in greater quantity by the French than by all other contingents of the Allied armies combined, Remarque describes hungry Russian prisoners of war trading knick-knacks with German peasants for food. "Our country people are hard and crafty when they are bargaining. They hold the piece of bread or the sausage right under the Russian's nose until he goes pale with greed, he rolls his eyes, and he'll agree to anything."

Serious artists created work of more significance. Fernand Léger painted one of his best pieces on the lid of an ammunition box. "Two days ago I pinched from an enemy a Mauser rifle," the sculptor Henri Gaudier-Brzeska wrote to Ezra Pound. "Its heavy unwieldy shape swamped me with a powerful image of brutality. I was in doubt for a long time whether it pleased me or displeased me. I found that I did not like it. I broke the butt off and with my knife I carved in it a design, through which I tried to express a gentler order of things, which I preferred."

This figure, a stylized mother and child, was one of his last works. He was killed in 1915.

*I*f troops did appear cheerful, they may simply have been drunk. "The 1914–1918 war made everyone drunk," Gertrude Stein wrote. "There was never so much drunkenness in France as there was then, soldiers all learned to drink, everybody drank." Just as Gallieni intuited that taxi drivers might cooperate more readily when supplied with the rough *vin rouge* known as *pinard*, officers in the trenches understood their men needed alcohol to sustain their morale and find the courage to go "over the top." A postcard intended for circulation strictly among the troops showed a grinning old soldier clutching six bottles of looted *pinard*. "With this," he says, "we'll give them a good hosing."

Each *poilu* carried two 1-liter *bidons*, or canteens. One generally held water mixed with red wine. The second contained tafia, a cheap rum from Haiti, distilled from molasses after the sugar's been extracted. Quality rum was aged in wooden casks to improve the flavor and disperse such poisons as fusel oil. In the process, it lost some of its alcohol. Tafia, sold straight from the still, retained all the impurities, as well as a ferociously high alcohol content: in most cases 100 proof—60 percent alcohol. The test of potency was simple. One mixed a few spoonfuls with gunpowder and dropped in a match. If it was the good stuff, it exploded.

According to a history of Haiti, "This rough spirit without finesse was nevertheless effective in its principal objective: to get pirates and the first colonists drunk." It did as good a job for the *poilus*. Officers not only encouraged drinking tafia before an attack but sometimes doled out what they called *un gout de rendre fou*—a drop to make you crazy. American Eugene Bullard, fighting in the Foreign Legion, agreed. "It made us more like madmen than soldiers."

Though the United States remained neutral until 1917, plenty of Francophiles volunteered earlier. Princeton alone sent 181 recruits, thanks to Presbyterian pastor Sylvester Beach, a former chaplain to Paris's American Cathedral. He hung Old Glory over the pulpit

each Sunday and led his congregation in singing "America the Beautiful." "In Princeton, we are all for war,"
he announced. Inspired, his daughter Sylvia, living in
Paris, volunteered as an agricultural worker, freeing a
farmer's son to fight at the front. Back in Paris after the
war, she opened the English-language bookshop Shakespeare & Company, which became an informal club-
house for former volunteers who returned to France as
the nucleus of an expatriate literary community.

Americans in Britain donated ambulances, and men
came from the United States to drive them. As well as
Ernest Hemingway, they included Harry Crosby, e.e.
cummings, Dashiell Hammett, and John Dos Passos, all
later successful writers, and also one Walter Elias Disney,
who found fame in another branch of the arts. Aside from
A Farewell to Arms, the war produced scores of novels,
hundreds of short stories, and unmeasured quantities
of verse. Cummings's imprisonment by the French for
three months in an administrative boondoggle inspired
his novel *The Enormous Room*. Harry Crosby, emerging
without a scratch from a front where all his friends died,
frenziedly celebrated his good fortune in Paris. He and
his wife Caresse electrified the city throughout the 1920s
and, almost as an afterthought, launched the tradition of
Paris expat publishing with their Black Sun Press.

Following a spate of panicky withdrawals from banks after mobilization, the French government froze all movements of funds in and out of France. Banks wouldn't cash foreign checks or travelers' checks or convert any currency. Even people with French bank accounts could withdraw only 5 percent of their balance, up to 250 francs. Those with a letter of credit were restricted to 25 pounds. "Nobody had any money," complained Nina Hamnett. "Paper money was refused everywhere. Only gold and silver were accepted."

The moratorium blocked those payments from home that kept many expats alive. At the same time, casual jobs dried up. The disappearance of tourists killed the market for guides, translators, even "dance partners"— gigolos. Nobody wanted English lessons anymore, and the need for relief waiters and *plongeurs*—dishwashers— shrank. With memories of how taxis had saved the city, the police also began confiscating private cars, putting chauffeurs, many of them foreigners, out of work.

The Chinese embassy on Avenue George V, just off the Champs-Elysées, must have appeared provocatively prosperous to the city's hungry Chinese students. Sixty of them invaded it that August, to find the ambassador enjoying his dinner. The sight of all that food

Police commandeering private cars, 1914

was too much. They politely ate his meal, then emptied the kitchen. The ambassador, who had been inclined to shrug off their plight, hastily cabled Beijing for additional funds to feed hungry nationals.

In Montparnasse, foreigners rallied round to support one another. The Russian painter Marie Vassilieff was more systematic than most. According to Nina Hamnett, "she started dinners in her studio at one franc fifty, with one Caporal Bleu cigarette and one glass of wine thrown in. We all went every evening and Modigliani too. A Swiss painter did the cooking." Along with other British nationals, Hamnett scraped together enough money to get to Dieppe, where ferries left for England. As none were running, the Brits were stuck there, often completely broke. Hamnett stayed in a cheap hotel with a whole girls' school, trapped on their way back from a tour of Switzerland. She lived on bread and cheese until boats began to run again. Arriving in Folkestone, she didn't have the money for a train to London. Fortunately, the British capacity for handling domestic disaster was unimpaired; stranded passengers were given tickets and billed later.

*I*n the first fervor of what looked like imminent victory, the hastily organized national groups that paraded with the French reservists had looked noble and inspiring. That rosy impression faded in the darker days of December as the ministry of war realized that amateurs, however well-meaning, might be more trouble than they were worth. Accordingly, it informed all foreigners who wished to fight that they would have to join the Foreign Legion, but that, in any event, enlistment couldn't begin until all French reservists were settled into their units.

In response, some formed private militias, hoping that disciplined well-drilled recruits would be more attractive to the army. Stranded Americans welcomed news of an American Volunteer Corps, members of which would be paid and, more important, fed. Recruitment began in a shop front under the colonnades of the Palais Royale. Today these former gardens of Prince Louis Philippe II, head of the Bourbon family, are a place of serene beauty, housing the Ministry of Culture and some of the most expensive boutiques in Paris. In 1914, however, the arcades surrounding them had deteriorated into a seedy backwater of crooked gambling clubs and a "meat rack" for prostitutes. Nevertheless, there was space in the gardens for troops to assemble, and for the American Volunteer Corps to parade and drill.

A journalist looking for the Corps' headquarters found it "crowded in between the shops of questionable jewelers and questionable booksellers." A limp American flag hung outside. Inside, three men distributed application forms to potential recruits. Some of the latter frowned over questions like "Why are you volunteering?"

"Because you love France," the journalist suggested, "and want to help in preserving her as the beacon-light of civilization?"

The recruit gratefully wrote this down, was signed up, and ordered to present himself at 8:00 a.m. every morning for drill. Only then did he ask the most important question.

"When is the grub going to begin on this deal?"

The American Volunteer Force faded away when the French army opened applications for the Foreign Legion. Tens of thousands applied, but only six hundred Americans were accepted. The small number suggests a calculated snub, particularly since it included men from South American countries and a few African Americans who chose not to enlist in the U.S. Army, since they were not, during the early days of the war, allowed into combat but used almost entirely as laborers. Among those accepted by the Legion was Eugene Bullard, a former boxer from Ohio who later became the first African American air ace.

Other than the trickle of volunteers for ambulance

and other noncombatant services, the United States would stay out of the war for three years. In 1914, those Americans destined to become its most famous combatants hardly knew the war was taking place. General John Pershing, later to command the American Expeditionary Force, was patrolling the Mexican border, chasing bandit Pancho Villa. He only took over the AEF when his predecessor died suddenly. Future air ace Eddie Rickenbacker hadn't even learned to fly. Alvin York was a drunken logger and railway worker in the backwoods of Tennessee. When he registered for the draft in 1917, the man who would become a legend for silencing 32 machine guns, killing 28 Germans, and capturing 132 more, cited religious objections to the war, scrawling laboriously on the recruitment form "Don't Want To Fight."

For three years, the promise of American manpower, industry, and above all money hung tantalizingly on the horizon, inspiring Europeans to both desire and despair. "God damn them!" wrote one exasperated critic. "Are they *ever* coming in? With their beautiful vainglorious talk. When is it reasonable to think the Americans will be able to put in that immense army of three million, fully equipped, each man with a hair mattress, a hot water bottle, a gramophone and a medicine chest?"

It wasn't until German submarines began systematic attacks on its shipping that, in April 1917, the United States reluctantly went to war. Even then, it was many months before its troops were ready to fight in France. Until they did, they clashed with British and Australian troops already fighting for two years or more and aggrieved by Russia's withdrawal. An Australian gunner wrote home in November 1917:

> *What do you think of Russia. The rotters have*
> *left us in the muck. They are worse than our strike*
> *leaders. Never mind Wait till the "Yanks" start.*
> *According to their guessing etc they intend to finish*
> *the business when they start. They can't beat our*
> *boys anyhow & they take care to keep their guessing*
> *to themselves when any are about. Half a dozen*
> *got poking muck at one of our infantry boys & he*
> *bogged right in & mixed things up till they cleared*
> *out.*

Meanwhile, American volunteers drove ambulances or ammunition trucks and observed the war like the tourists who would follow them after 1918. Malcolm Cowley described a moment when his unit found itself caught between French and German artillery. They took refuge in the grounds of an old château while shells roared overhead, "as if we were underneath a freight yard where heavy trains were being shunted back and forth." Cowley's evocation of the moment, except for the implication of some remote risk of injury and death, would not be out of place in any memoir of travel in rural France.

We looked indifferently at the lake, now empty of swans, and the formal statues chipped by machine-gun fire, and talked in quiet voices— about Mallarmé, the Russian ballet, the respective virtues of two college magazines. On the steps of the château, in the last dim sunlight, a red-faced boy from Harvard was studying Russian out of a French text-book. Four other gentlemen volunteers were rolling dice on an outspread blanket. A French artillery brigade on a hillside nearby—rapid firing 75s—was laying down a barrage; the guns flashed like fireflies among the trees.

If only someone had thought to bring a guitar.

19

G'day, Digger!

Fellers of Australier,
Blokes an' coves an' coots,
Shift yer bloody carcases,
Move yer bloody boots.
Gird yer bloody loins up,
Get yer bloody gun,
Set the bloody enermy
An' watch the buggers run.

C. J. DENNIS, *The Austra-Bloody-Laise*

And what about Archie?

Michael had been right about the National Archives in Canberra. It was almost embarrassingly simple to download a copy of Archie's military dossier, though decoding the twenty-page file of multicolored forms, peppered with rubber stamps and minutely annotated in

Troop ship leaving Australia, 1916

often unreadable handwriting, would have challenged an Egyptologist.

Poring over these documents with a magnifying glass, I did discover that, on October 7, 1916, Archie boarded His Majesty's Australian Transport *Ceramic* with five hundred other volunteers, for the voyage to Britain.

In a ritual that became familiar for all passenger ships leaving Australia, hundreds of relatives and friends gathered on the dock, each clutching one end of a long colored paper streamer held by a loved one on board. Pulling away, the ship stretched the streamers until they parted, the torn ends fluttering into the murky water of the harbor—a foretaste, though none could know it, of the mud and slush of the Somme.

By the standards of troop transportation, the *Ceramic* was superior. Only four years old, Belfast-built, she had speed enough to outrun German submarines, and two 4.7-inch guns to defend herself. All the same, the voyage was no tropical cruise. More than sixty years later, I came to Britain in almost the same way, creeping across southern oceans in a ship that seemed barely to move. Archie took even longer—forty-six days, against our thirty. We went east, stopping in Fiji, Acapulco, Miami, and both ends of the Panama Canal. The *Ceramic* headed west, along the hard-luck route dictated by places where they could take on coal: around the southern coast of Australia, across the Indian Ocean to Colombo, then through the Suez Canal, the Red Sea, the Mediterranean, or alternatively, via Capetown and Sierra Leone, but in both cases up the Atlantic coast of France to dock in Plymouth.

"We have to put our watches back about twenty minutes every day," wrote one soldier. "They alter the time on the ship at midnight so we get that much longer in bed." As each degree of longitude added a little to darkness and deducted it from the next day's dawn, Archie may have felt, as I had, a sense of Europe creeping over him like a thrilling sickness. He would have lain sleepless at night in his stifling bunk, only to nod off during the day—probably during droning lectures designed to keep out of mischief the wilder element among the volunteers.

The behavior of the Aussies rattled British officers. "They acted as if they were on holiday," said one—which, to many Australians, they were. Historian James Curran points out that

> *foreign wars have performed a valuable historical purpose in closing the cultural distance between Australia and the world. Between 1914 and 1919, Australian soldiers visited well-known tourist destinations such as Colombo, Cairo, London, Paris, Edinburgh, Belgium and Rome. At various stages they trained in the shadow of archetypal tourist landmarks such as the pyramids at Giza and Stonehenge. They documented their travels for those back home, bought postcards, took photos and collected souvenirs.*

Some volunteers had been itinerant shearers or fruit pickers in civilian life. To them, the army was a handy way to see the world at government expense. Others

Boxing match on board Ceramic

had migrated to Australia and looked on enlistment as a free ticket back home. Some were criminals. Every military unit attracts bad characters, but the AIF had more than most. Plenty of petty thieves recognized the opportunities for larceny in the confusion of war. Most of these volunteered without coercion, though some did so under pressure from a judge who offered the choice of enlistment or prison.

Seldom having taken an order in their lives, these men sneered at military discipline. Each troop ship had a prison, or "clink." They were never empty. Fights were common. Sometimes officers exploited enmities, giving two men boxing gloves and letting them duke it out for the entertainment of the rest, but generally the fights were bloody bare-knuckle affairs, private and vicious. Most involved theft. Systematic looting, known as "rat-

Two-up school, 1920s

ting," was commonplace. Any item left unguarded even for a few minutes could disappear, and soldiers learned to carry their valuables everywhere.

Gambling was rife. One officer described his vessel as "a regular Monte Carlo." Large sums changed hands at round-the-clock sessions of Housie Housie, aka Bingo, and Crown and Anchor, a Royal Navy favorite that used special dice and a baize mat marked out in squares for betting.

Nothing, however, trumped Two-up. As simplistic as a nursery game, Two-up has evinced an inexhaustible appeal to Australians at war. Two coins are flipped in the air, and bets laid on whether they land heads or tails uppermost. With its blanket spread on the floor, two big copper pennies with their "tails" sides marked with a white cross for easy identification, the wooden "kip" used to flip them, a "cockatoo" to keep watch, and the ritual shouts of "Come in, spinner!," the clandestine Two-up school is as emblematic of Australian service life as American craps.

Public gambling remains illegal in Australia, but on Anzac Day police ignore the Two-up schools that spring up behind every pub. In wartime, wise commanders also turned a blind eye, even when dishonest "tossers" rang in double-headed pennies, used superior mental arithmetic to shade the odds, or employed "stand-over men" or enforcers to extract their winnings. Better for an officer to be thought too lax, a "good bloke," than to be labeled a spoilsport, a "wowser," particularly since Australians took unkindly to discipline anyway.

In their eyes, a commander didn't lead by right of military law and the chain of command but with the approval of his men—an approval earned through experience. Of Australian soldiers, Peter Stanley wrote, "they could be led but not driven; would obey but also question. They would exercise their judgement; needed to be told not just what to do but why. They demanded a degree of freedom foreign to essentially regular armies like that of Britain."

Australian attitudes to authority were embodied in the song "Waltzing Matilda." Andrew Barton "Banjo" Paterson wrote it in 1895, and by 1914 it was well on the way to becoming an informal national anthem. Paterson was inspired by an incident in the 1894 strike of shearers. Notoriously anti-authority, they clashed with "squatters," ranchers who opposed trade unions. The owner of Dagworth station in Queensland led three policemen in a chase after Samuel "Frenchy" Hoffmeister, an agitator who had burned down his shearing shed. Cornered, Hoffmeister is supposed to have committed suicide, though a descendant of the dead man challenged that account in his own colorful brand of English.

The shearers camp nicknamed him as "Frenchy" was out of ignorance from his origines of being a german really from "Alsass Lorrein" and Berlin Germany where his family took him to live as a child! The Shearers (some couple men) of Murdered Samuel by shooting him in the open mouth while the other held him and then threw the pistol of "thiers" down by his side against that tree where his body was propped against until discovered!!!! So they got off with plain MURDER those bastard unionist because the police didnt do their jobs properly.

Paterson recognized the iconic power to Australians of a rebel who would kill himself rather than submit to authority. He made Hoffmeister a wandering tramp, a "jolly swagman," who kills a "jumbuck," or sheep. Ordered by the squatter and troopers to show what's in his "tucker bag," he quixotically leaps into the "billabong," the waterhole, and drowns.

Australian conceptions of discipline first clashed with British military law during the Boer War. After an ambush in which two hundred men died, a general called the All-Australian Victorian Mounted Rifles "a damned fat, round-shouldered, useless crowd of wasters; a lot of white-livered curs." When three soldiers answered back, then deserted, they were court-martialed and sentenced to be shot. British soldiers could be executed for more than a dozen crimes, but the Australian army didn't impose the death sentence. After a near-mutiny, General Kitchener commuted the sentences, then rushed the men back to Australia before they could serve them.

He was not so lenient with Harry "Breaker" Morant, bush poet, noted horse breaker, and a lieutenant in the Bushveldt Carbineers. Morant captured some Boers he believed had killed a comrade, and summarily shot them, as well as some complicit witnesses, under what he claimed was an unwritten rule condemning hostiles found wearing items of British uniform. At his court-martial, the British denied any such rule existed. Morant responded sarcastically that, in that case, he'd applied his own "Rule 303"—the caliber of the Lee-Enfield rifle. Memories of Morant's fate were still fresh when the first Australian volunteers sailed for Europe. On the *Ceramic*, the issue would have been as immediate as was the loss of Alsace to the French.

At every refueling port, scores of men disobeyed orders and sneaked ashore to find booze and women. In Colombo, capital of the future Sri Lanka, hundreds climbed down mooring ropes and were soon reeling drunkenly and, in some cases, half-naked through the town, though what really scandalized British officers was a rumor that a colonel dining at the Grand Oriental Hotel had found himself sharing a table with an Australian private and a stoker.

Rounded up the next day, the men showed no remorse. Too numerous for the clink, they were corraled on deck awaiting discipline, from where they derisively harmonized on "Rule Britannia," emphasizing the line that "Britons never ever *ever* shall be slaves." Some men never came back on board, bribing a local to hide them until the ship sailed. By the end of the war, four times more men had deserted from the AIF than from any other Dominion force.

Boredom and frustration led to clashes between the British and the Australians, who, at six shillings a day, were paid twice what a British Tommy received and were eager to spend it. Tempers frayed even more when, as happened increasingly, troops were ordered to shovel coal in African ports when local labor was short, were debarked before arriving in Europe, or, once they got there, held in reserve in so-called rest camps, where they did nothing all day but drill.

In December 1914, the first Australian volunteers, instead of going on to Europe, were kept in Egypt to relieve British troops guarding the Suez Canal. Cairo's brothel district, the Harret el Wasa', aka The Wazza, offered one of the few places to let off steam. In April and July 1915, already weary of the heat, the flies and the sand, they trashed establishments where they'd been cheated or robbed. The Australian government paid off the Egyptians and hushed up the disturbance, but similar clashes occurred wherever bored Australians were kept from what they saw as their rightful recreation.

Early in 1915, Australian poet Leon Gellert spent

seven weeks on a ship off the Greek island of Lemnos, waiting to go into battle on the Gallipoli peninsula. He vented his frustration in the poem "Dreams of France."

Oh, France, that I had ever dreamed of thee!
I thought to help thee bear the brandished lance,
But, lo, I sail the blue Aegean sea!
Sweet thoughts of thee still stand before mine eyes,
While I lie fettered in this stagnant cage;
Unseen by me the golden Grecian skies,
Forgotten is the Grecian Golden Age.
Drear and dank this stale Ionian bark
That plods its path along Aegean ways.

As much as he sounds like a Mediterranean cruise passenger moaning about the itinerary, the poem does express the sense of entitlement felt by Australian volunteers. They'd been promised a war, and they were bloody well going to get it, or know the reason why. Archie would have arrived in Europe with a similar belief that in return for his service, he was owed some excitement before he returned to the stodginess of life as a Sydney grocer, weighed down with the responsibility of a wife and family.

20

Die Fräulein

Careless talk lets vital secrets out.
You never know who's listening
To what you talk about.
PROPAGANDA SONG, World War II

The war forced Germany, France, and Britain, three countries intimately connected by bonds of family, culture, and language, into a messy divorce.

As Queen Victoria's husband, Prince Albert, had been German, many of their children married into European royal families, taking their Germanophilia with them. In 1917, George V of Britain changed the family name from Saxe-Coburg-Gotha to Windsor—a decision in which he lagged behind commoners in France, Australia, and the United States. In Australia, the town of Germanton had already become "Holbrook," and

German Creek "Empire Vale." The German shepherd dog reemerged as an Alsatian. Schmidts became Smiths and Brauns were transformed into Browns, although Hollywood character actor Gustav von Seyffertitz may have overreacted when he took the name "G. Butler Clonebaugh."

Britons lamented the disappearance of German sausage; a postcard circulated showing a large frankfurter wrapped with a black bow of mourning. In the United

The wurst is over

States, pretzels no longer appeared in bars. In a tradition revived in 2003 with "freedom fries," Americans rebaptised sauerkraut "liberty cabbage."

Professional terminology was thrown into chaos. How was one to forget that the leading news service was Reuters and a major banking family Rothschild? Baedeker produced the most reliable travel guides; X-rays were Roentgen rays; the test for syphilis was named for its inventor, Wasserman, and its treatment for its discoverer, Ehrlich. In botany, the fuchsia bore the name of its discoverer, Leonhart Fuchs, and the classic blue iris was actually *Iris germanica*. In music, Mozart's opus numbers were preceded by the letter *K* for the man who catalogued them, Ludwig von Köchel. The works of Johann Sebastian Bach could not be discussed without reference to the *Bach-Werke-Verzeichnis*, or catalogue of Bach's works.

In the short term, concert halls just dropped Bach, Beethoven, and Schubert from their programs, but a long history of German interest in music from all nations could not be erased. British composer Edward Elgar, for example, owed his reputation to an early vogue for his work among German audiences. He toured Germany, where he was lionized. Elgar never renounced that support, unlike France's Camille Saint-Saëns, who, in *Le Figaro* of November 14, 1914, disowned it.

> *I haven't forgotten that German artists often interpreted my work, that German theatres presented my opera* Samson, *that I accepted German decorations. Of all that, I'm aware. But so what? From now on, a river of blood and mud will separate us. I have no sympathy for people who treat as "scraps of paper" the treaties they have signed, who carry off to Leipzig the priceless treasures France and England have entrusted, who massacre women and children, who offensively advertise their intention to seize three- quarters of Europe. Some*

years ago I wrote, "Once I loved Germany; now I
fear it." Today we hate it, we execrate it, and with
good reason.

While France made the same cosmetic adjustments
to the language as other nations, a second problem was
more deep-rooted. Just as Anglo-Saxon families favored French maids and cooks, the French traditionally
hired governesses and nannies from Germany. Count-
less German ladies, middle-aged, unmarried, and plain,
joined French families as fräuleins. The type was so familiar that Abel Hermant could nail her in a thumbnail
sketch.

She's an alert young woman, a bit short and plump,
strapped into a corset, and dressed in the latest
style, simple, but with a hint of poor taste; a bit
old fashioned. On her head is that nameless thing
known in most languages as a hat. Very blonde,
naturally. A nasty look in a bland face. A cunning
look, as if of a conqueror. When she walks, she
doesn't advance—she captures terrain.

As soon as war broke out, the satirical magazines decided, with little or no evidence, that all fräuleins were

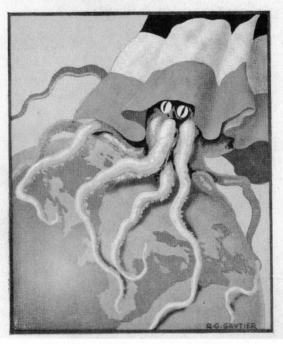

Exposé of supposed German espionage

Fräulein Spy

either propagandists for the Teutonic way of life, brain-washing their charges, or outright spies, or possibly both. *La Baïonnette* ran a striking cover by Fabien Fabiano of a mild-looking fräulein with her ear to a door.

In a cartoon, another is asked by a friend, "So you're

a governess in Paris? Who do you work for?" She replies, "The Wilhelmstrasse." An elaborate double-page spread shows a German nanny ordering a terrified French child to grovel before a beefy Wagnerian heroine in long braids and a crown, while behind her a confederate is sweeping out the treasures of European fantasy—Puss in boots, Pierrot, Don Quixote, Santa Claus.

*E*vidence of spying among fräuleins was sparse, but propagandists made up for that in speculation, as they had done in fabricating stories of atrocities in Belgium. These claimed Germans systematically cut off the hands of children, while their officers indulged in drunken mass rapes. There was no reliable evidence of either. "The invasion of Belgium," noted one historian, "with its very real suffering, was nevertheless represented in a highly stylized way that dwelt on perverse sexual acts, lurid mutilations, and graphic accounts of child abuse of often dubious veracity."

These tales appeared even in such staid technical journals as the *Annales des Maladies Vénériennes*—The Annals of Sexually Transmitted Diseases. One described Belgian girls kept in stalls like domestic animals for the pleasure of "a squad of hussars." In another, officers supposedly chose the fifty prettiest girls of a town and locked them in a barn with fifty soldiers. Any who didn't submit were eviscerated. An even more fantastic report in the *Chronique Médicale* claimed that a German officer took over a church, herded in all the available women, barred the door and celebrated a profane mass, drinking champagne from the sacred vessels. After this, he orchestrated an orgy. Any woman who resisted had her throat cut or was crucified, following which the Germans locked the door on their victims and set the church on fire.

Well-meaning journalists were often taken in, particularly since propagandists were skillful at setting the scene. Marie Louise Mack, an Australian amateur, bluffed her way into occupied Belgium in 1914 and described what she saw in her book *A Woman's Experiences in the Great War.* Though she encountered nothing more terrible than German rudeness and officiousness, her imagination made up for it.

> *I had been used to think of the German race as tinged with a certain golden glamour, because to it belonged the man who wrote the Fifth Symphony; the man who wrote the divine first part of* Faust.

Oh, Beethoven, Goethe, Heine! Not even out of respect for your undying genius can I hide the truth about the Germans any longer.

What I have seen, I must believe!

They took me to the church. On the high altar stand empty champagne bottles, empty rum bottles, a broken bottle of Bordeaux, and five bottles of beer. In the confessionals stand empty champagne bottles, empty brandy bottles, empty beer bottles. Stacks of bottles are under the pews, or on the seats themselves.

The sacred marble floors are covered everywhere with piles of straw, and bottles, and heaps of refuse and filth, and horse-dung. The Madonna's head has been cut right off. They have set fire to the beautiful wood-carving of our Saviour, and burnt the sacred figure all up one side, and on the face and breast.

A dead pig lies in the little chapel to the right, a dead white pig with a pink snout.

And now we come to the Gate of Shame.

It is the door of a small praying-room. Still pinned outside, on the door, is a piece of white paper, with this message in German, "This room is

private. Keep away." Inside are women's garments,
a pile of them tossed hastily on the floor, torn per-
haps from the wearers.

"Perhaps" is the operative word. Was the room anything more than a place where clothes were kept for dis-
tribution to refugees? Could the Germans really have
emptied all those bottles themselves? And why store
them in a church? No matter. As the propaganda theo-
rist Harold Lasswell explained, "a handy rule for arous-
ing hate is 'If at first they do not enrage, use an atrocity.'
It has been employed with unvarying success in every
conflict known to man."

The Scholar

And still they gazed, and still the wonder grew,
That one small head could carry all he knew.
OLIVER GOLDSMITH, *The Deserted Village,*
1770, describing the village schoolmaster

 $\mathcal{W}$ here will you go?" friends asked as I headed
for London on the track of Archie's time in
England. "The Imperial War Museum?"

"Eventually. But not right away."

They looked skeptical. "You've got another source,
as good as the Imperial War Museum?"

"Better," I said.

The farther north you go in suburban London, the
less you feel you're in Britain. In the 1930s, European
refugees settled on these tree-lined streets in Victorian
apartment blocks, known as "mansions." Squint and

The Sage of Golders Green

you could imagine yourself back in Simmering, Licht-
enrade, or some other district of Berlin or Vienna. Con-
ductors on buses about to enter this alien world of deli-
catessens, kosher butchers, watchmakers, and old men
in cafés playing chess would yell jokingly, "Next stop
Swiss Cottage. Passports ready, please."

The sense of another country intensifies in Golders

Green, of all these suburbs the most *mittel European*. Although the tide of new arrivals from Iran, Syria, and Lebanon has diluted the sense of a corner of some foreign field that is forever Dusseldorf, the presence of a vast cemetery and crematorium stand as reminders of why so many people crossed the Channel to make a new home here.

Neil is from emigrant stock; his family fled pogroms in Russia to settle here in the 1880s and take up the very European trade of tailoring. The stamp of that culture has long since faded, however. Tall, upright, bearded, brusque, Neil could only be English. In his theatrically modulated voice I hear Rex Harrison as the sea captain who haunts the coastal cottage of Gene Tierney in the film *The Ghost and Mrs. Muir.*

In one respect, however, Neil's roots remain deep in European soil. He's an example of that respected, even revered individual, the scholar.

Such people study for the pleasure of acquiring information. They may use what they discover as material for writing or teaching, but most are driven by the pure urge to *know.* To pass a bookshop without browsing, to visit a house without looking at its books, to meet persons of adventurous ways and not coax them for anecdotes would never enter their head.

Scholars choose professions that leave them free to

wander off for weeks on end. For Neil, that was performance. Busking his way across Europe as a young man fed his tireless intellectual curiosity. Back in Britain, he formed a small acting group called Phantom Captain that directed the spirit of inquiry into theatrical projects: a musical based on particle physics, for instance, and *Loaded Questions*, a show that carried the scholarly impulse to surreal extremes by consisting entirely of questions.

In his early seventies, he still performs. In 2010, he could be found doing street theater at the Shanghai Expo, for which he invented *Krikitai Chi*, a tai chi–like slow-motion version of cricket without bat, wicket, or ball.

Occasionally he appears as a solo act, often in bizarre personae. For one festival, he dressed as a tramp in scuffed shoes, shapeless felt hat, and seen-better-days suit and hung a sign round his neck advertising "Lick You All Over—One Pound."

Looking at a photograph of this bedraggled creature—ever the scholar, Neil documents everything, even his humiliations—I asked, "How did it go?"

"Quite well for a few hours. Everyone seemed to get the joke. But then one woman actually gave me a pound and demanded I do as promised."

"And . . . ?"

"Put it this way. By the end, I felt I'd fully explored the possibilities of the role."

We were talking in Neil's study, halfway up the rambling apartment he occupies with his wife in Golders Green. The number of levels remains a mystery: the upper reaches are inaccessible to all but Neil, the staircase walls lined by shelves jammed with books and the landings piled with objects too bulky to place elsewhere.

I stumbled over one of these on my way to the bathroom: a life-size bust of a young woman, shoulders draped in a real lace shawl. Next to it was another head, of a beaming man with flowing mustache, topped with a Chinese cap, also real.

"Shop window dummies?"

"Ah, no. The remains of an experiment, actually." Neil brushed the dust from the man with the mustache. "This is supposed to be me. They're wired for sound. When they're working, one can have a conversation with them—or at least appear to. I thought of using them in a theater piece, but it never quite worked out." He pointed up the flight of stairs toward the bathroom. "Watch the chain. It's a bit tricky."

When I got back to his study, the coffee table in the middle of the room was piled with card folders, brown manila envelopes, and ring-back binders.

"These are a few World War I things I thought might be useful."

The term "primary source" has a special magic for the researcher. A clear Xerox copy or scan of an old and faded document may be easier to read, but there is no substitute for the original. To feel the texture of the paper and smell the dust is to hear the scratch of the pen that wrote it, the clack of the typewriter, the thump of the rubber stamp, and, through them, to achieve a psychic contact with those who created it.

A museum might give me access to superior copies of what Neil showed me. But they were no substitute for the real thing. Respectfully I opened a plastic envelope.

Popular Songs of the A.E.F, a tiny booklet on cheap brown paper, barely larger than a playing card, published by the YMCA in 1918. On the yellowing water-stained cover, I could just read the words "Give me the man who goes into battle with a song in his heart."

A song in your heart—in the mud of the Somme? What bloody fool said that? And yet, to read these titles is to feel a link no history can convey. "If You Were the Only Girl in the World," "Keep the Home Fires Burning," "Love's Old Sweet Song." For soldiers far from home, songs, even as sentimental and trite as these, have always been the ultimate repository of emotion.

"Strange," mused Noël Coward, "how potent cheap music is."

A second envelope contained another booklet. *My First Week in Flanders* by Lieut. the Hon. W. Watson Armstrong, 1/7th Northumberland Fusiliers. Privately printed in London in 1916. Water-stained also, though printed on better paper than the YMCA booklet. Lieutenant *the Hon*? Only the children of viscounts, barons, and earls may style themselves "the Honorable." I leafed through it.

> *One shell, which burst a yard or two off me, killed two of my men and injured another. The two men displayed great heroism in their dying agony. One of them, Bob Young, as he was carried away, minus his legs, called upon an officer, who was almost overcome by the sight, to be a man; and I was further told that he died kissing his wife's photograph, and with the word "Tipperary" on his lips. . . .*

Next, a phrasebook without cover. Phrases appeared in English, then in French, then in a phonetic version. At random, I opened it at "Care of the Wounded."

"I feel very tired." Je suis très fatigué. Je swee tray fateegay.

"I am cold." J'ai froid. Jay froah.

"I am suffering very much." Je souffre beau-coup. Jer soufr bok-koo . . .

Minus his legs, he called upon an officer to be a man . . .

Neil said, "And I thought this might be of interest."

A battered lump of a book, its thick brown cover, chipped at the edges, bore the label:

Salmon's
Popular Series of
Patriotic Post Cards

The binding had long since ceased to contain its bulging contents, a collection of colored postcards, each glued down to a page. I knew of Salmon of Sevenoaks as a major postcard publisher. I was holding a sample book carried by one of its salesmen. He'd have shown it to stationers and tobacconists who wanted to order cards.

I eased off the elastic band that kept it together. Cards spilled out, some detached from the page: the symbolic figure of John Bull in top hat and Union Jack

Guess I'll go and fight the Germans too.

For the Old Flag.

waistcoat, with a truculent bulldog at his side; languid youths playing tennis or billiards when they should be at war; a cringing but sneering kaiser, mustache drooping, *pickelhaube* on his head. Archie might have seen these cards in the newspaper kiosk on a drafty railway station as he endured the hurry-up-and-wait of military life. There he is. A tall, diffident man in a khaki greatcoat and flat military cap. Cautious eyes: asking a favor of a stranger never comes easily to Australians. *Would you have a cigarette, mate?*

"So," said Neil. "Any of this useful?"

"Oh, yes," I said, closing the book. "Yes, indeed."

On the Secret Shelf

Mademoiselle from Armentières, Parley-voo?
Mademoiselle from Armentières, Parley-voo?
Mademoiselle from Armentières,
She hasn't been kissed in forty years,
Hinky, dinky, parley-voo.

HARRY CARLTON AND JOE TUNBRIDGE,
popular song of the Great War

A researcher is a pack rat, a private eye, a grave robber, a ghoul. I've collected all my life, both to acquire material for books and for the pleasure of accumulation. Two garages overflowing with books, magazines, posters, documents, and letters give proof of a persistent fascination with the hunt. My appetite whetted by Neil's material, I put my nose to the ground and began the search in earnest.

To scavengers, the street markets of junk known as *bro-*

cantes are the truffle groves of information. Any weekend, we can be found rummaging through cartons of papers, boxes of postcards, heaps of magazines, sifting through the sand of society for flecks of informational gold.

Over twenty years of haunting *brocantes* and junk markets on three continents, I'd seen thousands of items relating to World War I: everything from medals and pieces of uniform to postcards and flower vases made from cannon shells. Some I'd even bought—in particular copies of magazines such as *La Baïonnette* and *L'Illustration*. Such magazines would be a good place to start my research, but to have some sense of how the war progressed, I needed more than isolated copies. Only long runs told the story in any detail, and these, I assumed, would be rare.

The first inkling that I was wrong came the following week. At the weekly street market at Porte de Vanves, I found a few wartime copies of *L'Illustration*.

"I don't suppose you have any more?" I asked the seller.

"Sure." He led me to his van parked behind the stand and opened the back doors. It was filled with cartons—including one that contained, as far as I could judge, a complete run of wartime issues of *L'Illustration*.

"How much?"

"Each?"

"For the lot."

"The lot?"

"I'll give you fifty euros," I said.

"Okay!"

He was hardly able to believe his luck. Back numbers of *L'Illustration*, like *Reader's Digest* or *National Geographic* in the United States, are almost unsellable. He was more than willing to carry them to the car, even at the risk, to judge from his bowed legs and red face, of a double hernia.

After that, it was a kind of gold rush. Maybe it was just because I was actively looking, but forty-four copies of *La Baïonnette* appeared on a market stall five minutes' walk from my home. Marie-Dominique located a run of *Le Miroir* from 1914 to 1916. In the seaside village where we have our summer home, she also spotted a pile of *La Vie Parisienne* and persuaded the dealer to reserve them until I arrived.

Seeing my delight, the dealer said, "It's material about *la guerre de '14* you're looking for?"

"Well, yes. In general."

He glanced around to see we weren't overheard.

"Are you interested in *unusual* stuff?"

"How unusual?"

He went digging in the back of his store and returned with two plain envelopes.

One contained six photographs. Three were postcards. In the first, a woman lies in bed, dreaming of her soldier lover, who appears in a balloon above her head. In the second, the man himself arrives outside her window, complete with tin hat, rifle, and greatcoat. In the third picture, he's discarded his kit and she's pulled back the bedding to welcome him in. Since such postcards generally came in groups of eight, I could imagine what happened next.

The other images were original photographic prints.

Two showed a young man carrying a rifle, with fixed bayonet, and wearing a military backpack. He looked embarrassed—understandably, since, unless you counted a wispy mustache and a willing expression, he wore nothing else.

The last photo was the strangest of all. Where the others had been, to some extent at least, professional, this one was homegrown. I could imagine the amateur photographer sloshing the print through developer and fixer in his home darkroom and grinning in satisfaction at how well it had turned out.

It showed the rear view of a nude woman, bent over, presenting her backside to the photographer. He'd

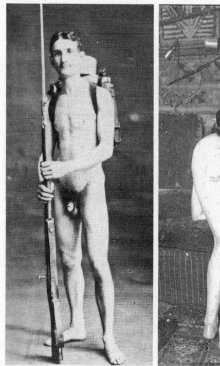

drawn on her buttocks a likeness of Kaiser Wilhelm and, to complete the *tableau vivant*, balanced a *pickelhaube* on her hips.

Trying to assume a scholarly expression, I said, "Interesting. Do you know when they date from?"

He pursed his lips. "About 1910, give or take."

He was guessing. But if these photographs did date

from before the war, it added a scrap of evidence to Peter's theory that France was preoccupied with things military long before mobilization.

"This came from the same place," he said, interrupting my thoughts. From the second envelope, he extracted a small folded square of cream-colored fabric.

"Do you know what it is?"

I did, as it happened.

Before vulcanized rubber made condoms cheap, men put their trust in kid leather, a pig's bladder, or a square of finely woven fabric—cotton or, even better, silk. Silk squares were produced for this purpose. They even inspired a joke. "He's a fine boy," a man says, admiring a friend's new baby. "He should be," replies the father sourly. "He was strained through a silk handkerchief."

"Yes. I've seen them," I said.

Not to be trumped, the stall holder said, "Not like this one."

He held it up to display its startling feature. It was photographically printed with pornographic scenes of monks and nuns in impious rapture and unecclesiastic dishabille.

Even the toughest *poilu*, from a lingering piety, might have shunned such an item, but a foreign soldier—someone like Archie—could well have bought it while on leave, and carried it, somewhat shamefacedly, in a wallet; confirmation for pals back home, if he ever got there, that France lived up to its reputation. Weren't condoms in their folded paper packets called "French letters" and oral sex known as "Frenching"? Sex was just one more thing, like baking bread or making cheese, at which the French excelled.

The dealer looked at me expectantly.

"I don't know . . ."

"If you take everything," he said, "I can make it . . ." He named an obscenely inflated price.

The postcards and photographs had no historical value. As for the handkerchief, who knew when it dated from or whence it came? Any serious historian would dismiss such material. But was it any different than the brass matchboxes, the vases hammered from shell casings? "Trench art" could encompass anything that reminded soldiers of the real world just over the horizon—fragments to cling to amidst the dirt and terror of war.

I reached for my wallet.

· 23 ·

Archie Under Arms

You see, but you do not observe.
SIR ARTHUR CONAN DOYLE,
A Scandal in Arms, Sherlock Holmes speaking

I chose a café for my next meeting with Peter van Diemen. It spooked me to think of sharing a glass of wine in our home with someone who, however much provoked, had beaten a woman to death.

The prejudice was irrational, I knew. Of the many people we'd entertained over the years, a few no doubt had blood on their hands. But they'd killed in war, not, as Peter had, in the heat of domestic argument. A uniform made all the difference—that thought was running through my head as I stepped out of the August heat and into the cool.

From a table next to a window opening onto rue de

Seine, Peter raised his head. I sat down opposite. We solemnly shook hands. *With that very hand. . .*

"Had any luck?" I asked hurriedly.

"Well . . . I did discover a few things."

This was no surprise. The more obscure the subject, the more there rises from its experts the unvoiced cry, "Use me!"

Reaching under the table, he took something from an open briefcase and placed it between us: a dark blue concertina file, half filled with papers, and neatly labeled on the front "Baxter, William Archie."

"All that?"

It surprised him that I was surprised. "Oh, there's more. I just couldn't carry it all."

"I'm astonished."

"Why? The Australian archives are very thorough."

"Even so, I never expected . . . from just those few documents . . ." *Who would have thought the old man had so much blood in him?*

"A document can be very revealing, and a photograph even more." He slid out the portrait of Archie and Stella.

"For instance?"

"The uniform, for a start. His tunic, the boots, the cap, the puttees. . . ." He pointed to the thick woolen bandages wound around his calves. "These tell us he was infantry, not cavalry, artillery, or signals. The records confirm this. His battalion, the Thirtieth, was entirely foot soldiers. Mainly in supply or reserve."

"What about the slouch hat we found?"

Descriptions of the Australian Light Horse charge at Beersheba in 1917, the last cavalry charge in military history, made me wonder if Archie might have been one of General Harry Chauvel's "forty thousand horsemen."

"Ah, yes. The hat." Peter leafed through the papers in the concertina file and extracted a sheet. "The assistant curator of heraldry and technology acquisitions at the War Memorial. Very sound chap. He sent me details of the items you deposited with them: a hat, a pistol, some ammunition . . ." He read for a moment. "Hat size, $6\frac{1}{8}$ inches. So it couldn't have belonged to your grandfather."

"Why not?"

"Too small. You can see from the photograph. He was a big man. That's probably why he's wearing a cap. They issued those when they had no hats in the correct size. Big sizes ran out first. No, the hat wasn't his."

"What about the pistol then?"

"I'm afraid not." He consulted the memo from the War Memorial. "'The Dreyse semi-automatic pistol captured by Private William Archie Baxter. . . .' I know the Dreyse. I have one, in fact. It's a German gun, 9.65 mm, issued to officers. It made a good souvenir because it was small. You could hide it in the bottom of a kit bag, under the dirty clothes. Nobody dug down that far."

So Archie was a scavenger, a ratter. It seemed that every serviceman was a pilferer. All the same . . .

"Did you find out anything about his actual service?"

"A great deal, as it happens. The Medical Corps also kept good records."

The Medical Corps! "So he *was* wounded? In the family there's a tradition that he might have been gassed."

Of all weapons, gas was the most insidious. According to one account, "the skin of victims of mustard gas blistered, their eyes became very sore and they began to vomit. Mustard gas caused internal and external bleeding and attacked the bronchial tubes, stripping off the mucous membrane. Fatally injured victims sometimes took four or five weeks to die." Novelist Vera Brittain, who worked as a nurse, wrote, "I wish those people who talk about going on with this war whatever it costs could see the soldiers suffering from mustard gas poisoning. Great mustard-coloured blisters, blind eyes, all sticky and stuck together, always fighting for breath, with voices a mere whisper, saying that their throats are closing and they know they will choke."

But Peter shook his head impatiently. "Gassing? No, nothing like that at all."

Archie's stature was diminishing before my eyes, like a sand castle eroded by the tide.

"His legs, then?" I said. "Everyone agreed he never walked easily again after the war. He must have suffered *some* kind of injury."

"Now that *is* possible."

Peter extracted a pink sheet from his file, headed "Casualty Form Active Service." I remembered it. The mixture of typed entries and variously readable handwriting, in colored inks that had differentially faded, had baffled me. Obviously he had more luck. Or maybe he just tried harder.

"This is your grandfather's entire medical history." He ran down the list with a pencil.

" 'Debarked from S.S. *Ceramic* Plymouth 21 November 1916.' Well, you knew that. Then the following day, 'Marched into Codford.' Codford was a transit camp on Salisbury Plain. Most new arrivals didn't have much military experience, so they'd have drilled there for a few weeks and got used to army discipline. '30 Decem-

ber Proceeded O/seas France SSO *Princess Clementine.*'
The *Princess Clementine* always sailed from Folkestone
in Kent; hundreds of thousands of troops crossed the
Channel on her. '6 January 1917. T.O.S'—that's 'taken
on strength'—at Etaples. It means your grandfather
was accepted for service in the front line."

"So where did they post him?"

"Well . . . as a matter of fact, nowhere."

"Nowhere?"

"Not *literally*. But nowhere in military terms. On
January 27 he was admitted to hospital in Etaples and on
February 10 evacuated back to England."

"He was wounded in camp?"

"No, not wounded. You said he had problems with
his legs. That's correct. But it wasn't related to combat.
He was suffering from varicose veins."

24

Dressed to Kill

*There were two fronts; there was the war front, and
then in Paris there was what might be called the
Montparnasse front.*

JEAN COCTEAU

Imprisoned by asthma in his apartment at 102 boulevard Haussmann, Marcel Proust wrote at night,
sleeping by day in his cork-lined bedroom, and only
rising, if he got up at all, at four in the afternoon. He saw
the war in fragments: glimpses through the windows of
his closed car as his chauffeur, Odilon Albaret, a former
cabbie and husband of his faithful housekeeper, Céleste,
drove him to some nocturnal rendezvous, sometimes
in the glitter of the Ritz Hotel dining room on Place
Vendôme, on other occasions to the small and squalid
Hôtel Marigny on rue de l'Arcade, a gay brothel man-

aged by Albert Le Cuziat. As Proust was a partner in the business, M. Le Cuziat willingly accommodated his sadistic tastes, which "needed," in the words of arch-gossip Cocteau, "the spectacle of a young Hercules slaying a rat with a red hot needle."

Seeing the city in time lapse alerted Proust to minute changes in style. Patriotism, he saw, was transforming fashion.

> *As the Louvre and all the museums were closed,*
> *when one read at the head of an article "Sensational*
> *Show," one could be certain it was not an exhibition of*
> *pictures but of dresses. Just as artists exhibiting at the*
> *revolutionary salon in 1793 proclaimed that it would*
> *be a mistake if it were regarded as "inappropriate by*
> *austere Republicans that we should be engaged in art*
> *when the whole of Europe is besieging the territory of*
> *liberty," the dressmakers of 1916 asserted, with the*
> *self-conscious conceit of the artist, that "to seek what*
> *was new, to avoid banality, to prepare for victory by*
> *developing a new formula of beauty for the generations*
> *after the war," was their absorbing ambition.*

With designers such as Patou and Poiret working for the army, smaller dressmakers and milliners flour-

Uniform chic

ished, particularly if they could improvise. Deprived of feathers from Africa and the Caribbean, Coco Chanel adapted the simple straws and berets of her country childhood. Like almost everything she did, they started a trend and increased her reputation. With silk unobtainable, dressmakers scavenged what they could. Once it became known that each flare sent up to light no-man's-land included a small silk parachute to slow its descent, soldiers on both sides risked their lives to retrieve them for their girlfriends back home. Two could be sewn into a pair of knickers, and four made a good-sized blouse.

*M*eanwhile, in Paris, shrewd designers suggested to their all-too-suggestible clients that it was their duty to dress well, so long as their clothes included some acknowledgment of the war. In a *Baïonnette* cartoon, a dowager asks a couturier if selling expensive clothes in wartime is unpatriotic. "Are you saying I'm not a patriot, Baroness?" he replies indignantly. "But who created the gown in Pekin taffeta called 'Croix de Guerre,' and the 'Where Will It End?' evening coat?" Proust noticed that

> *young women were wearing cylindrical turbans on their heads and straight Egyptian tunics, dark and very "warlike." They were shod in sandals, or puttees like those of our beloved combatants. Their rings and bracelets were made from fragments*

1915 fashions—the military look

of shell casings from the 75s, and they carried
cigarette lighters consisting of two English half-
pennies to which a soldier in his dug-out had
succeeded in giving a patina so beautiful that the
profile of Queen Victoria might have been traced by
Pisanello.

Soldiers on leave in Paris, expecting to see many women in mourning, were told the custom of wearing black for a year after the death of a loved one had been allowed to slide—"the pretext being," wrote Proust, "that [the deceased] was proud to die—which enabled them to wear a close bonnet of white English crêpe (graceful of effect and encouraging to admirers), while the invincible certainty of final triumph permitted them to substitute satins and silk muslins for the earlier dark cashmere, and even to wear their pearls."

Better than trench-art accessories or having your dressmaker run up a military-looking costume was winning the right to wear a uniform. The first stop for anyone with the slightest connection to an ambulance service or to the armed forces was, as had been the case with Misia Sert, their tailor or dressmaker. The Regent Tailor on boulevard de Sebastopol offered to create "military uniforms in satin, suede, leather, whipcord, gabardine, khaki etc. Cut and styling beyond reproach." For those who couldn't afford made-to-measure, plenty of stores offered ready-to-wear. In Henri Barbusse's novel *Under Fire*, a *poilu* on leave in Paris is dazzled by "the shop windows displaying fantastic tunics and *kepis*, cravats of the softest blue twill, and brilliant red lace-up boots." The New America, a manufacturer of military wear in bulk, advertised, "Wholesalers, department stores and tailors etc. who would care to contact us will receive an immediate proposition that will allow them to double their business in a week."

Edith Wharton, paying a visit to the front, noted the diversity of uniforms.

> *The question of color has greatly preoccupied the French military authorities, who have been seeking an invisible blue, and the range of their experiments is proved by the extraordinary variety of shades of blue, ranging from a sort of greyish robin's-egg to the darkest navy. . . . But to this scale of experimental blues, other colours must be added; the poppy-red of the Spahis' tunics, and various other less familiar colours—grey, and a certain greenish khaki, the use of which is due to the fact that the cloth supply has given out and that all available materials are employed.*

The inconsistency of fabrics and the proliferation of uniforms from other countries and armies helped draft dodgers to lose themselves. In *Le Feu*, five soldiers from the front notice that some of the men who appear, from a distance, to be soldiers, are actually wearing a kind of fancy dress. Arriving home on leave, writer Paul Tuffrau was as astonished by the gaiety of the women on the boulevards as by the dubious military credentials of their men.

> *The lighted department stores, the beautiful cars,*
> *the pretty girls in their little hats, high-heeled boots,*
> *rice powder, muffs and little dogs, and draft dodgers*
> *in beautifully tailored blazers and breeches that*
> *look like uniforms, but drip with gold braid brighter*
> *than anything on the jackets of real officers. Over*
> *and over, you see such sights, next to soldiers on*
> *leave who roam the boulevards in tin hats, muddy*
> *greatcoats and heavy boots.*

In John Dos Passos's novel *Three Soldiers*, an American on leave is overwhelmed by the variety and quality of the uniforms in the cafés around the Opéra, none of them damaged or stained by combat. "Serbs, French, English, Americans, Australians, Rumanians, Tcheco-Slovaks. God, is there any uniform that isn't here? The war's been a great thing for the people who knew how to take advantage of it." Songwriter Cole Porter owned an entire wardrobe of uniforms. His friend Monty Woolley recalled, "Porter had more changes than Maréchal

Foch, and wore them with complete disregard to regulation. One night he might be a captain of the Zouaves, the next an aide-de-camp."

Young common soldiers, embittered by their experience of the front, found the city's cynicism disgraceful. In June 1916, Gaston Biron wrote to his mother at the end of a leave, "You will probably be astonished to hear that it was almost without regret that I left Paris, but it's the truth. I've noticed, like all my comrades who are left, that these two years of war have, little by little, made the civilian population selfish and indifferent, and that we and the other combatants are almost forgotten. So what could be more natural than that we become as distant as they are, and return to the front calmly, as if we had never been away?"

In September, at Chartres, Biron died of wounds. He was thirty.

After leaving the ambulances, Cocteau joined a fortnightly magazine called *Le Mot*—The Word. Like most publications in Paris, it was geared to the war. Part of his job, not so different from that of Norman Lindsay in Australia, was to demonize Germany: in his case, to produce sketches of imaginary atrocities committed by the Germans in Belgium, including children whose right hands had been hacked off. Fortunately, enough was happening in Paris to take his mind off these squalid tasks.

Literally and figuratively, he had a new love, aviation, and in particular a young military pilot, Roland Garros. Already famous at twenty-seven for having been the first aviator to cross the Mediterranean, Garros downed four German planes with a new system of aerial gunnery he helped develop. Born on the Indian Ocean island of Réunion—Cocteau called him "my dear creole"—Garros boasted the slight frame, dashing mustache and dark complexion of action star Douglas Fairbanks, one of Cocteau's childhood heroes. At school, Cocteau took gymnastic classes in hopes of emulating his feats. Garros was married, but he and Cocteau discovered a mutual attraction. The pilot took Cocteau up for joy rides, an experience the poet found all the more dizzying for their infatuation.

*P*aris could not help but find war *chic*. Just as dressmakers were not content simply to get by with inferior materials but adapted them into a new style, hostesses embraced austerity and offered only a token apology for dinners of soup, bread, and wine. Who cared, so long as there was good talk?

As Malcolm Cowley had noticed, privation and danger stimulated the creative juices. Cocteau flitted around the city, attending benefit concerts for the troops, posing for portraits, and socializing with his old patron, Misia Sert, while cultivating such glamorous newcomers as the Princess Hélène Soutzo, fiancée of diplomat-writer Paul Morand. As he did so, he was incubating an idea for something new: a ballet for Diaghilev's Ballets Russes, now based in Rome. In 1912, while the Ballets Russes was appearing in Paris, he'd pressed the impresario to let him write something ambitious for the company.

Diaghilev is walking home after a performance, his thick underlip sagging, his eyes bleary as Portuguese oysters, his tiny hat perched on his enormous head. Ahead, Nijinsky is sulking, his evening clothes bulging over his muscles. I was at the absurd age when one thinks oneself a poet, and I sensed in Diaghilev a polite resistance. I questioned him about this and he answered, "Astonish me! I'll wait for you to astonish me."

Cocteau believed he had found such an astonishing idea. It would take only passing account of the war. One might almost think of it as thumbing its nose at the news by dwelling on the silliest aspects of reality. As he wrote just before the premiere, "Our wish is that the public may consider this as a work which conceals poetry beneath the coarse outer skin of slapstick. Laughter is natural to Frenchmen: it is important to keep this in mind and not be afraid to laugh, even at this most difficult time."

He had already suggested to a producer of Shakespeare's *Midsummer Night's Dream* that members of the Fratellini clown family play the "rude mechanicals." Now he thought of an entire ballet based on the traveling circuses that toured country carnivals. Before such shows, performers appeared on a small stage outside the tent in excerpts from the program, while barkers shouted the attractions of each and urged the audience to pay and see the full show: "Step right up: it's all happening on the inside." Both the stage and the performance were called a *parade*.

Erik Satie, whom Cocteau knew from Misia's salons, agreed to write the music. As for the costumes, he must have the gruff, opinionated Pablo Picasso, who could have returned to neutral Spain like many of his compatriots but preferred to remain in Paris. Composer Edgard

Varèse offered to introduce them. For the occasion, Cocteau arrived at Picasso's Montparnasse studio dressed, in tribute to the clowns in his paintings, as Pierrot.

Picasso was easily persuaded to collaborate on the ballet. Shrugging off the war and ignoring the fact that he hated to travel, he took the train to Rome with Cocteau to pitch their idea to Diaghilev. By the time they arrived, they'd decided broadly on the action and style. Against a vivid backcloth of carnival themes, characters in cubist costumes would dance the story of three circus acts *en parade*. One would be based on movie serial daredevil Pearl White; another on Charlie Chaplin. There would be a pantomime horse, and (don't tell Satie) gunshots, sirens, and other noises, the shouts of the barkers spoken through a megaphone, and a passage played on water-filled milk bottles. They called it *Parade*.

25

Misery Hill

For it's Tommy this, an' Tommy that, an' "Chuck
him out, the brute!"
But it's "Saviour of 'is country" when the guns begin
to shoot;
An' it's Tommy this, an' Tommy that, an' anything
you please;
An' Tommy ain't a bloomin' fool—you bet that
Tommy sees!

RUDYARD KIPLING, "Tommy"

*Y*ou're not seeing it at its best," said Wilf, my
guide.

Shoving frozen hands into the pockets of my water-
proof jacket, I pulled my ears deeper into the collar and
turned away from the wind. Sleet rattled on my back
like birdshot. As I shook my head, more water flew off

my hair and eyebrows than one would expect from a good-sized Airedale.

"Really?" I tried not to sound sarcastic.

Back in the 1970s, I'd lived three years in East Anglia. Our front yard was the North Sea, our nearest neighbor Norway. Wind and rain of dismaying intensity and persistence swept across Suffolk and in particular Norfolk, the most prominent attribute of which was immortalized by Noël Coward in his play *Private Lives*.

> *Elyot (of new wife): I met her at a house party in Norfolk.*
> *Amanda (ex-wife): Very flat, Norfolk.*
> *Elyot: There's no need to be nasty.*

Wiltshire, in which we stood, was on the far side of Britain from Norfolk. Naïvely, I'd expected it to be as I remembered it: a county of stately mansions; a disciplined eighteenth-century landscape, rational and discreet, dotted with *faux*-Greek follies in white marble. But I'd visited here only in summer. In winter, Wiltshire's weather gave Norfolk a run for its money.

How had it looked to Archie when he arrived here in November 1916?

Perhaps the flat winter landscape, gray and wet, with its leafless trees and pale diffused light, so different from the blistering blue-white of Australian sunshine, aroused in him the same mingled excitement and dismay as when, more than sixty years later, I walked, shivering in my too-thin clothes, into the center of Southampton, where our ship had docked the night before. But how much worse for him and the other volunteers to learn, as they came ashore, of the Battle of the Somme, which had ended just the week before—a four-month campaign by the Allies that gained almost nothing but, on the British side alone, left 420,000 men dead.

Wilf steered me into the shelter of a large oak. From around the massive trunk, I peered into the murk, across the little one could see of the featureless plain. Cold had numbed my face like Novocain.

"What's over there?" I asked, looking west.

"Artillery range."

"And there?" Looking east.

"Same." A sweep of his eyes took in most of the horizon. "It's almost all army. Has been for more than a century."

"No farms?"

For an answer, he hacked at the sodden grass with

the heel of his Wellington boot. A divot of turf peeled away, revealing, an inch beneath the surface, the gleam of white.

"Chalk. The whole plain's the same. Nothing grows here but grass. Army got it cheap. Anyway, the amount of unexploded ordnance buried in this piece of country . . ." He grimaced. "Even if they let you plow it, you'd probably blow your leg off at the first furrow."

We drove back to Codford in Wilf's mud-spattered SUV, bumping along a track that was mostly a set of parallel ruts brimming with muddy water. In peacetime, a pretty enough village of five hundred people, a single main street, its gray stone church of Saint Mary the oldest and largest building within miles, Codford had been transformed by the time Archie arrived. Three thousand Australians and New Zealanders were quartered across a shallow valley on the edge of town, living in wooden huts and rows of conical white tents.

I could see why the army chose it. Plenty of open country, a railway spur, and the river Wylye nearby. Not much agriculture, so fewer civilians to be upset by a mob of bored and unruly soldiers on the doorstep. Not many big towns to distract the troops: fewer places for them to get into mischief. During both wars, Salisbury Plain was dotted with camps. Their names turned up repeatedly in memoirs of Australians in Britain—Fovant, Hurdcott, Codford, all within fifty miles of where we stood.

Wilf led me on a squelching tour of the former campsite. I was glad of my borrowed Wellington boots. Pictures from 1917 showed horse-drawn carts bogged to their axles in mud. It wasn't any dryer now.

"Why didn't they put it up on the chalk?"

His deadpan look with raised eyebrows, an expression as typical of the British as the French shrug, signaled that I'd asked something a true countryman would have known from simple observation.

"Too far from the railway and the river." He nodded in the direction of the Wylye and the bridge over it. "There wasn't enough mains water, so they used the river for washing—and . . ."

I got the dangling "and." Three thousand men and not enough lavatories to go round: no fun for the people living downstream.

"Very little to do around here, back then," I said.

"Not much to do here *now*."

"Pubs?"

"A couple. Australians liked our dark bitter, a lot stronger than the lager you drink out there. If you

wanted lighter beer, the camp canteen sold it in bottles."
He paused. "There *was* a tottie too, I'm told."

"A prostitute? Just the one?"

"A place like this, the locals wouldn't have tolerated
more. In France, maybe, but not in England. Anyway,
she gave everyone the clap, I'm told."

More likely they gave it to her. Though Codford
mainly existed to toughen up new arrivals from overseas
and casualties returning to France, it was also a convalescent camp for gonorrhea and syphilis victims. Soldiers
feared a "dose" more than a bullet wound, since any sufferer lost all pay and privileges while being treated. And
the army made a point of telling your family what was
wrong with you.

A shaft of watery sun lit the hill behind the camp.
Patches of grass and earth had been cleared off the chalk
to create a kind of picture. Such carvings cropped up
all over the chalk downs. Locals had been making them
since the Stone Age. Horses were a popular subject,
though the most famous was the Cerne Abbas Giant,
a huge man, club in hand, sprawled across a hillside,
penis arrogantly erect. According to local custom, even
the least fertile woman would conceive if she passed the
night within the circle of one of his enormous testicles.

Rising Sun Badge, Misery Hill, Codford

"It's not old," Wilf said of the Codford design. "1917. Almost overgrown now. Can you make it out?"

Briefly, as the sun struck it, I recognized the rising sun of the Australian army badge. I nodded.

"Misery Hill," he said.

"Pardon?"

"The squaddies called it Misery Hill. It was a punishment. Defaulters were sentenced to dig on it. There were so many brown beer bottles around the camp that the squaddies filled the trenches with them, bottom uppermost. When the sun hit, they made the badge look like it was made of bronze. But nobody can be bothered to keep it up now."

A moment passed in silent contemplation. This had been no holiday camp. As much as anywhere in Flanders or on the Somme, it felt drenched in despair.

I thought about Archie. Leaving a bleak, flat, blisteringly hot and dry landscape, he'd landed in a bleak, flat, freezing cold and wet one. From the little I knew of him, he didn't seem the kind of man to relish the irony. Particularly not if he was suffering from varicose veins. A chronic affliction of people who spend a lot of time on their feet, the condition occurs when poor circulation in the legs prevents blood from moving back up the body. As it pools in the calves, the veins swell and bulge, becoming knotted, blue, and twisting. Trudging Sydney streets every day, visiting clients to take their orders, Archie would have been a classic sufferer.

How could the medical examiner in Sydney have failed to notice something so obvious? According to historian Bill Gammage, the standards were demanding. One man "was told that his eyesight was defective and was twice turned away before a £2 tip facilitated his passage into the Australian Infantry Force. Rejected men stumbled in tears from the tables, unable to answer sons or mates left to the fortunes of war. They formed an Association, and wore a large badge to cover their civilian shame."

Perhaps, as the flow of recruits dried up, doctors didn't look too hard. Unlike poor eyesight, varicose veins wouldn't stop you from firing a gun. Or possibly the weeks of drill, first in Sydney, then at Codford, brought it on. Either way, his arrival in England derailed Archie's war.

After three hours, I'd seen everything Codford had to show. If it was boring to me, how much more so for the men stationed here? Particularly when the war ended and they wanted to go home.

"It was in '18 that things got rough," Wilf said. "Repatriation took forever, and the men just lost it. Their officers couldn't control them. The MPs were sent in, but your mates just beat them up. Then they deserted. Stopped cars on the road and made them take them into Salisbury. Or women drove out here and camped in the woods. And remember that local prostitute?"

"What about her?"

"The chaps she infected . . . some say they dragged her out of her house and threw her down the town well."

"Seriously?"

He stared up at a sky as gray as cement.

"Like I said—not much to do around here."

26

Bedside Manner

Nursie, come over here and hold my hand.
Nursie, there's something I don't understand.
'Round my heart there's a funny little pain.
Oh Oh Oh Oh it's coming back again.

ART NOEL AND DON PELOSI,

"Nursie, Nursie"

As Archie lingered in Codford Camp, unsure of his future, the privations of the war had begun to bite in Paris. In 1913, philosopher Charles Péguy complained that "the world has changed less since Jesus Christ than it has in the last thirty years." He exaggerated, but Parisians, seeing their creature pleasures disappearing one by one, must have nodded in agreement.

Changes began almost at the moment France mobilized. In 1914, the government outlawed absinthe, claiming it sapped the will of young Frenchmen to fight.

"Absinthe makes you crazy and criminal," ranted one ill-informed journalist, "provokes epilepsy and tuberculosis, and has killed thousands of French people. It makes a ferocious beast of man, a martyr of woman, and a degenerate of the infant. It disorganizes and ruins the family and menaces the future of the country." The sentiments were less shocking than the way they were expressed. Before the war, no writer would have been so immoderate.

The absinthe ban was an omen. As breweries and vineyards converted to making alcohol for military use, the quality and quantity of wine and spirits declined. Coffee, imported from Africa and the Caribbean, became unobtainable. Dried and pulverized chicory root, initially used to stretch coffee, completely replaced it.

Cigars disappeared. Cigarettes followed. Most *poilus* smoked pipes filled with a shag they called *perlot* or *gros cul*—big ass. Each soldier received a free weekly ration, but it became so adulterated that it could barely be coaxed into flame. "You should use it to thatch cottages," suggested one soldier drily. "It would cut down on the work of the fire brigades." Even matches, made to austerity standards, wouldn't strike. Once the United States entered the war, the shortage of cigarettes became acute. A poster showed an obviously strung-out marine

pleading with the folks back home: "I Need *Smokes* More Than Any Thing Else."

In *La Vie Parisienne* for February 1915, George Barbier, known before the war for his fashion drawings and scenes of oriental exoticism, took a hard look at wartime Paris. In three images, he illustrated "The Parisienne in 1914." In the first, she's cavorting at a formal ball in a plumed hat and daring off-the-shoulder gown. The second shows her doing a spirited tango with a beau dressed in *le smoking*. In the third, she's taking leave of him the next morning. She's outfitted for the street, but he's still in his pajamas.

"The Parisienne in 1915" is more sober. She indulges in charity, giving a coin to a beggar. We see only a patched cuff, but it's enough to telegraph his need. Everywhere one looked in Paris, someone was asking for money. Panhandlers—usually refugees, plus a few deserters and draft dodgers—proliferated. So did sellers of charity badges. "I have been pestered by thousands of women selling flags for some charitable [sic] cause," wrote a facetious correspondent to the trench newspaper *The Wipers Times*. "Yesterday, a forward female had the audacity to ask me to buy a flag to assist in the purchase of a blue body-belt for a bucolic Belgian. Only last Sunday I gave a franc to provide Warm Woollens for War-worn Walloons."

The last of Barbier's impressions is also the most revealing. It shows the Parisienne following one of the few patriotic pursuits appropriate to a lady of fashion— nursing.

*I*n the first days of the war, U.S. ambassador Myron T. Herrick suggested to the French surgeon general that Americans in Paris form their own ambulance service. The general proposed instead that they convert a school, the Lycée Pasteur in the upmarket satellite suburb of Neuilly, into a five-hundred-bed military hospital entirely staffed by their own volunteers. He probably thought they would never be able to agree among themselves, and that the labor supply, if any, would quickly dry up. In fact, women flocked to Neuilly. One journalist wrote:

> *They came dressed in their best frocks and hats. The physician in charge was businesslike from the beginning.*
>
> *"I want women who would come at eight o'clock in the morning and stick to the job all day long, and who can be counted upon to come every day."*
>
> *"I can come every day from two to four," said one.*
>
> *"I could never get away out here before ten in the morning," said another.*
>
> *"I can come mornings, but must leave at half past eleven," said a third.*

Suspecting the sincerity of some applicants, the doctor shrewdly asked, "Which ladies are available to nurse wounded officers only?" Two-thirds stepped forward—to be rebuked: all servicemen, other ranks and officers both, were entitled to the same care.

Worthy in theory, this wasn't practical. Officers, wealthier and better educated, were bound to receive more careful attention from nurses, most of whom came from the same class. *Poilus*, resentful of this, sometimes expressed their dissatisfaction by greeting the arrival of amateur nurses on the ward with a coordinated cannonade of farts. Even when enlisted men welcomed visitors from the upper classes, the intellectual gap yawned. *La Baïonnette* showed a member of the Académie Française, the country's highest repository of learning, struggling to talk to a private with the help of a *poilu* dictionary.

Enthusiasm for nursing diminished after the 1915 execution of British nurse Edith Cavell. The Germans were within their rights to condemn her. She never denied helping prisoners to escape and passing military information to the Allies. The British and French shot just as many, including the hapless Mata Hari. Cavell made an end worthy of Marlene Dietrich, who would play a female spy shot by a firing squad in the 1931 film *Dishonored*. Cavell's execution inspired one of the most

George Bellows. The Murder of Edith Cavell

vivid artworks of the war, a 1918 painting by American George Bellows. It shows a slim, pale, almost ethereal figure descending into the yard where her brutish, slovenly captors wait to kill her. No less hagiographic, the best known of her many monuments, next to London's Trafalgar Square, is engraved with her last-night-on-earth statement; "Patriotism is not enough, I must have no hatred or bitterness towards anyone."

In death, Cavell became what she had never been in life—a star. In Britain during the weeks following her death, enlistment in the armed forces doubled. Even so, a firing squad was not what every mother wished for her child, and the dilettantes melted away, diverted into less hazardous tasks, such as making baby clothes for the children of men at the front and knitting socks and sweaters.

Knitting was enjoying a vogue, thanks in part to Edith de Beaumont, who encouraged it as therapy for the wounded. With wool in short supply, she asked a friend in New York for help. After the *New York Times* published her letter, the countess was inundated with wool—all put to good use, as she summarized, somewhat in the condescending manner of Lady Bountiful, in a second letter, published in January 1916.

> *If you could only see the happiness and realize the service this has rendered—all the poor women to whom I have been able to give work, some of them mutilated, some having only one leg. The men, too, are working, those who are infirm. We teach these poor creatures how to knit, and they can make socks. Those who have been long months in bed, inactive, all their work goes to the front where it is most useful. A large convoy of wagons that my husband has organized is just leaving for Saloniki [Gallipoli], in which are quantities of warm woolen things, socks, and shirts for the wounded.*

*The fantasy of nursing . . .
and the reality*

The disappearing nurses were replaced in the wards by tough ladies, mostly French, who didn't flinch from their often grim work. Hospital administrators weren't sorry to lose the amateurs, particularly the pretty ones. The liaison of Ernest Hemingway and his nurse Agnes von Kurowsky that inspired *A Farewell to Arms* was hardly the last affair between patient and nurse. Just as its erotic opportunities drew Jean Cocteau to ambulance work, some nurses signed up with an eye to romance, even just sex. *La Vie Parisienne* showed a slim white nurse standing between two husky and grinning black Zouaves with the caption "A black-bread sandwich."

As the French government, anticipating thousands of casualties, allocated millions of francs to their care, speculators smelled profit. By 1915, the French Red Cross was staffing fifteen hundred hospitals, and after that, the number only grew. Strapped for cash, owners of châteaux too expensive to heat and maintain offered them as hospitals, knowing their upkeep would be paid by the government. Abandoned by the Russian grand dukes and the crowned heads of the Austro-Hungarian Empire who had been their most reliable clientele, luxury hotels along the Mediterranean such as the Carlton and the Negresco became convalescent homes.

Profiteering knows no racial boundaries, but it suited France's institutional anti-Semitism to suggest most speculators were Jews. For *La Baïonnette* in August 1917, Paul Iribe showed Jewish and black African gamblers scooping up their winnings in the casino that the nation had become. Elsewhere, a Jewish shopkeeper reports that, while most business is down, his "Maison X" is doing well. Maison X sells artificial limbs.

Exploiting the handicapped was a lucrative business at every level. The same July, police found "a mountain" of unworn but mismatched shoes in the apartment of a trader at the weekly market on boulevard Richard-Lenoir. He'd stolen them from displays in shoe stores, which only ever showed one shoe of a pair. Security was lax in such stores—who would want only a left or a right shoe? In fact, the man's market business specialized in selling individual shoes to amputees.

The greediest exploiters of the wounded were not unscrupulous Jewish merchants but their own comrades, who looted the belongings of those careless enough to leave them unguarded. In particular, the male nurses and stretcher bearers of the Royal Army Medical Corps became so notorious for larceny that soldiers suggested the initials RAMC stood for "Rob All My Comrades." According to historian Peter Stanley, one serviceman "lying ill on a stretcher at Boulogne, about to board a hospital ship for Britain, watched helplessly as an orderly sorted through his bag, taking his money and souvenirs."

The novelist Colette was scandalized that people who contributed nothing to the war should have profited so much from it, and in particular from the care of the wounded. Her novel *The Last of Chéri* dissects the postwar decline of fashionable Paris, contrasting the complacency and greed of profiteers with the despair of those who returned from the war damaged in body or spirit.

That the speculators make their money from medicine seemed to her particularly cynical. In the novel, retired courtesans invest the proceeds of their dissolute lives in clinics and health resorts. The wife of former boy-toy Chéri manages a hospital partly owned by Americans, while his one-time *protectrice*, Léa, now middle-aged and overweight, has put her money into a mineral spa. Chéri, himself wounded at the front, is alone in pining for the gracious days before the war, and once he's convinced they are gone forever, he shoots himself.

❉ · 27 · ❉

The Way to Kiss a Mary

While you're living in the bright lights with the
merry and gay
There's a loving heart you've broken just to pass
the time away
And she is more lonesome, more lonesome than you.

LOU KLEIN AND HARRY VON TILZER,
"There's Someone More Lonesome Than You"

The cooperation of French, British, and colonial soldiers that functioned in the trenches seldom worked so well at command level, where it clashed, screeched, and seized up periodically like a rusty machine. Many British and American officers regarded fraternization with the French as disloyalty, even treason. The poet e. e. cummings and a friend spent four months in a French prison camp after an officer decided cummings's antiwar sentiments, his speaking French, and his friend-

ship with French officers suggested he was a spy. Some Allied officers believed arrogantly that they were there to show the slovenly French how war should be fought. Lionel Lindsay, brother of Norman, drew a notably undiplomatic sketch in which a jovial koala bear in trim AIF kit and slouch hat consoles a bedraggled, battle-worn poodle wearing the tattered uniform of a *poilu*.

Well-meaning French people made things worse by attempting to explain concepts they didn't understand. "The whole world knows the famous 'Tipperary,'" wrote one journalist. "Civilians think it's a cheerful song, bouncy and gay. How wrong! It's slow and melancholy, particularly when the voices descend about the middle of the refrain." A Parisian music hall

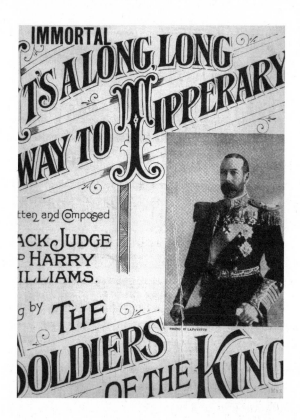

picked up on this idea and, inspired by the death of Edith Cavell, presented a dramatized version, sung mournfully as the singer is marched to her death. "Good-bye, Piccadilly," she sobs as the shots ring out. "Farewell, Leicester Square!" The French audience couldn't understand why Britons among them were laughing.

Australians and Frenchmen who managed to become friendly discovered more affinities than differences. "Mateship," for example, had always been regarded as a uniquely Australian institution. That *poilus* could regard a *pote*, or pal, with similar esteem initially surprised Australians, then became the basis of an enduring understanding. An issue of *La Baïonnette* devoted to *les potes* contains numerous images redolent of Aussie mateship: soldiers spoon-feeding injured friends or sharing the last puffs of their pipe. Other sketches were more melodramatic. "Why did you jump in front of me when they fired?" asks a soldier of his wounded comrade. "Because you have kids," he replies. In another, the sergeant demands of a corporal, "Why did you risk your life to save a dead man?" The man says, "He was my *pote*." One didn't need to explain such decisions to Australians. They would do the same for one of their mates and not think twice.

Prudish staff officers particularly disapproved of the complaisant French attitude to sex and banned the erotic magazines produced for its troops. They singled out *La Vie Parisienne* and the pinups of its most popular artist, Raphael Kirchner, an émigré from Austria and therefore, in their eyes, a potential fifth columnist.

La Vie Parisienne *cover by Kirchner*

To Australians, this was yet another infringement on their already circumscribed liberty. One of them, Frank Molony, wrote in his diary:

> *In this morning's orders, Kirchner [was] pronounced anathema, and* La Vie Parisienne *declared beyond the pale. In a word—trading with the French in indecent pictures and literature is forbidden. The "indecent pictures" referred to are*

of the French—photographs of the nude—and of beautiful courtesans certainly, so beautiful that only rarely can the terrible word "indecent" be used toward them, but the literature! Considering the only doubtful literature sold to the Troops by the Frenchies comes from well-established London publishers, this order is quite in keeping with their damned hypocrisy and pettiness.

Postwar novels, films, and songs like "How Ya Gonna Keep 'Em Down on the Farm After They've Seen Paree?" give the impression that numerous American servicemen took leave in Paris. In fact, very few Allied soldiers ever saw the city. They were given little enough leave to start with: five days a year, if they were lucky. Most Britons and Australians spent it in Britain, where they didn't face the barrier of language, but Americans were forbidden to do so unless they had blood

relatives there. As their bases were far to the east, in the Argonne and Savoie, doughboys were urged to take their leave in such regional centers as the sleepy spa town of Aix-les-Bains.

The first Americans to spend a furlough in Aix-les-Bains were taken straight from the front for that purpose and, to their collective surprise, whisked there en masse in a public relations exercise. The YMCA, which handled leisure activities for the American Expeditionary Force, orchestrated a lavish reception. The Aixois did their best to make the first contingent welcome. Flags were flying and locals cheered as the grubby and bemused doughboys paraded through town. Their hosts had even scraped together a baseball team; "the nine in white linen trousers, red jerseys, bare heads and knees and American flags tied about their arms stood with chattering teeth and trembling legs for two hours." That evening, the former casino, now converted into a club for soldiers on leave, presented a show by vaudeville performers from London, and the African American musician and composer James Reese Europe, identified simply as "Europe," led the band.

Stars and Stripes described the events under the optimistic headline "Fresh from Trenches to Delights of Aix." Its reporter worked hard to boost Savoie, "that little wedge of pure beauty that keeps the Alps from slipping down into the broad plains of northern Italy." He explained that both Queen Victoria and J. P. Morgan sampled the baths of Aix and enjoyed its hotels, seventy of which, with a little arm-twisting, had agreed to accept doughboys as guests.

The reporter insisted that Aix promised a pleasant, if not terribly dramatic leave: "hikes on the mountains, motor boat trips on the magnificent lakes, auto trips, billiards and other games, a library, reading, writing, and lounging rooms. As warm weather comes there will be added outdoor recreations—golf, tennis, squash." Pleasant enough—but for a young soldier hoping to accumulate enough memories for a lifetime, a hot bath, a soft bed, and a good book were not what he was looking for.

Allied troops stationed farther west had a better chance of seeing Paris, but not before they were thoroughly indoctrinated. The historian James Curran wrote:

> *Upon arrival in Paris, Australian soldiers*
> *were taken directly to Caserne de la Pérpinière*
> *barracks for lectures on the dangers of VD and for*
> *distribution of prophylactics and treatment aids.*
> *This was also where leave passes were stamped to*
> *confirm arrival, which annoyed the soldiers, many*

*of whom dodged the trip. It was unpopular for two
reasons. First, the Anzacs resented the lectures
concerning the horrible effects of venereal disease:
they had already seen enough bodily mutilation in
the trenches, and the sordid details in the lectures
gave the impression that even the prospect of
pleasure could be spoiled. Second, the lectures stole
valuable time. Because Paris leave was so prized by
the troops (even though it was usually for only four
or five days, half the time allotted to London, or
"Blighty," leave) and also because it was initially
open only to officers (whose pay it was thought could
more easily cover the expense of Paris leave)—
these incursions into an already truncated period
of time infuriated the troops. Their response was to
intensify their leave period, to compensate not only
for the lack of time, but also for the possibly limited
lifespan they faced as soldiers. For this, Paris would
prove to be the perfect environment.*

Those that did get there spent their time in Paris
mostly visiting museums, parks, and monuments: the
Louvre (when it was not closed for the duration), the
gardens of the Tuileries, the Palais de Justice, the Bois
de Boulogne, described by one soldier as "Paris's Hyde

Park," the Eiffel Tower (though fenced off and adapted to radio transmissions), the cathedral of Notre Dame, even the military museum at the Hôtel des Invalides, and sometimes the Palace of Versailles.

As few ventured into Montparnasse, Montmartre, or the working-class areas locals called *Panam*, the lives of typical Parisians remained an enigma to them. When they speak of the French in their letters, it's seldom by name. Those they do describe are the *bourgeoisie* of central Paris, whom they would know only from seeing them on the street or in a café. Women were invariably admired from a distance. One Australian wrote:

> *I never saw a really plain girl all the while I was there, neither did I see a thick pair of ankles. Invariably small in build, they are dainty without exception, with large languorous eyes, both blue and brown, lashes that lay upon their cheeks as it were, noses aquiline, sensitive and artistic, mouths small with moist red lips, rounded, well moulded chins and nearly always a dimple in each cheek. When they talk, they do it with their eyes, and when they smile it is the same, their conversation is full of music, it is just delightful to listen to them. Only small it's true, but they are just bubbling over with*

*the very joy of life, chock full of spirits and enjoying
love and passion to their utmost capacity.*

Guides put out of work by the disappearance of the
tourist trade preyed on the soldiers, steering them
to the same clip joints they'd taken civilians to before
1914. One group of Australians fell into the hands of a
guide who claimed to have worked for the prestigious
Thomas Cook travel agency.

> *We dived into a back street and went into the As
> de Coeur—Ace of Hearts. It was a dirty shop with
> a couple of naked (except for shoes, stockings and
> a flimsy silk scarf) women flitting about in it.
> They sat on fellows' knees and carried on generally.
> We had a drink and departed. The next place
> was Les Belles Foules—The Beautiful Fowls
> [actually, Aux Belles Poules: poule corresponds
> to the English "chick"]—slightly higher in tone.
> Numbers of half dressed girls were here. They went
> on with some disgusting dances and foolery. Next
> place we took taxis to. It was an exhibition such as
> might grace a back street in Cairo, but something
> that I did not believe could be seen in Paris.*

Paris brothel, 1917

Less squalid companionship was available to the personable visitor if he knew where to look. The bars of such music halls as the Moulin Rouge, Concert Mayol, and in particular the Folies Bergère were well-known pickup spots. An Australian who visited the Folies in March 1917 disapproved of the show's suggestiveness, but also of the "working girls" of the *promenoir*.

> *On the whole the show may be described as rotten. At the back is the promenade a very brilliant sight and nearly the whole audience repair there between the acts to stroll and listen to an orchestra there. Throngs of girls—some very beautiful—infest the place and persistently keep pestering you, clinging*

on to belt and having to be beaten off almost. The performance on the stage would not have been toler- ated in Australia, first on account of its dirt (which had not even the redeeming grace of smartness) and secondly on account of its absolute weakness [i.e., lack of humor].

Most of the songs and gags were in French. The only bright spot was at the last when all lights were turned out and a girl appeared in the air sitting in a chariot on the end of a long pole. This was thrust right over the audience and her feet brought just above the heads of the audience. There was great competition to get her shoes and eventually she lost them both. When the show terminated we set off for home and had to run the gauntlet of guides & girls which took not a little negotiating.

Less predatory women cruised the upper lounges of larger theaters such as the Châtelet and Théâtre du Champs-Elysées. For a few francs, any one of them would take a man back home, or to an *hôtel de passe* that rented rooms by the hour.

Military officialdom equated promiscuity with pros- titution, but some women were just looking for a good time. Canadian writer and longtime Paris resident Mavis

Gallant has written of "that mute invitation [that] used to be known as, '*Suivez-moi, jeune homme.*' [Follow me, young man.] It was the prerogative of married women. The unmarried were chaperoned, or didn't dare, or were semi-professional—which means to say, just now and then, hoping just for a good dinner in a decent restaurant, a cab home, a bit of cash."

Women encountered in this way expected no more than for the man to pay for a meal and the room, and perhaps "buy them a new hat"—the polite formula for a small cash gift. Most were more than satisfied with the arrangement. *La Baïonnette* published a cartoon of a young English private putting on his trousers while his companion of the night says coyly, "I wish there were more 'contemptibles' like you."

Encounters like this were common among soldiers on leave in Britain, where language was not a barrier. In France, to meet a woman required basic French. Officers enjoyed the advantage of higher education and could often speak the language, whereas, even after months in France, the average Tommy or Aussie knew little more than *Promenez avec moi?* (Walk with me?), *Couchez avec moi?* (Sleep with me?), *Parlez-vous?* (Do you, or will you, speak to me?), Toot sweet (i.e., *tout de suite*, immediately), and the all-purpose *Bon* (Good).

Discouraged by their officers from learning the language, they developed a form of Franglais that further mangled communication. To them, the town of Ypres, which the French pronounce something like "Eepr," looked like "Wipers," which is what they called it. There was even a trench newspaper called *The Wipers Times*. Trying to order wine in a café and hearing the French ask for *vin blanc*, Australians misheard it as "plonk," which became, and remains, Aussie slang for wine of any sort.

Once the Americans arrived, language became a bone of contention. Doughboys resented what some saw as an unwillingness on the part of locals to learn "American." As for learning French themselves, its grammar and pronunciation seemed to them perversely misleading. In one of his invented letters home from baseball player cum doughboy Jack Keefe, humorist Ring Lardner had him describe his problems with his French tutor.

For inst. he asked me what was the English word for very in French so I knew it was tres so I said tres and he says no it was tray because you say the letter e like it was the letter a and you don't pay no attention to the letter s. So I asked him what it was there for then and he said that was just the French

*way of it so I had a notion to tell him to go and take
a jump in the lake but I decided to say nothing and
quit.*

The few British and Australian soldiers who found
French girlfriends then had to adjust to their more so-
phisticated sexual habits. In his memoir *Good-bye to All
That*, Robert Graves, a captain in the Royal Welsh Fu-
siliers, wrote of his fellow officers, some of whom spoke
French:

> *A good deal of talk in billets concerned the peculiar
> bed-manners of Frenchwomen. "She was very nice
> and full of games. But when I said to her: 'S'il vous
> plaît, ôtes-toi la chemise, ma chérie,' she wouldn't.
> She said: 'Oh, no'-non, mon lieutenant. Ce n'est
> convenable.'"*

"Please take off your blouse, my dear." "Oh no, my
lieutenant. That's not appropriate."

Gradually hints of new tastes crept into the jokes
and songs sung by Tommies and Anzacs. In particular,
a Tipperary parody signaled the arrival of cunnilingus
on the Anglo-Saxon sexual menu.

That's the wrong way to lick a Mary.
That's the wrong way to kiss.
Don't you know that over here, lad,
They like it best like this.
Hurray pour les Françaises.
Farewell Angleterre.
We didn't know how to tickle Mary
But we learnt over there.

The Cure for Cockroach

"Don't be alarmed, Cinderella," said the fairy. "The
wind blew me your sighs. I know you would love to go to
the ball. And so you shall!"
CHARLES PERRAULT, *Cinderella*

Every Paris magazine aimed at a male reader-
ship carried, next to listings of "rare and artis-
tic" books and photographs, columns of classified ads
for prostitutes. Most were disguised as offers of mas-
sages, baths, and manicures. Typically, "Miss Mohawk
of New York" promised "hygienic care, expert manicures, English and Canadian massage and scientific
treatment. A first class house."

After 1915, a new category of advertisement joined

them. In column after column, soldiers appealed for *marraines de guerre*—godmothers of war—who would write them letters, send them little comforts, and invite them home during their leave in Paris. Typically, Corporal Lorin of the 166th Infantry, stationed at the fortress of Verdun, "desired to establish relations with an affectionate, young and pretty Parisienne."

Officers had an edge; doctors and fliers even more. An "aviator in convalescence before returning to the front" appealed for "a pretty *marraine*, spiritual and loving." Some played the soul card: "Poet, at the front since the beginning, suffering from *cafard*, requires a *marraine* between 25 and 30." *Cafard*, literally "cockroach," was *poilu* slang for the boredom and depression brought on by idleness—during which, it was said, men in the trenches passed the time taking potshots at the plentiful roaches.

The *marraines de guerre* were an instant success. Women's magazines published suggestions for suitable "comforts" to send adopted godsons. Most women contented themselves with knitted socks and scarves, though so many of these were received that aid agencies often unraveled them and sold the scarce wool to buy items the troops really needed. One journal proposed a practical use for the rabbit skins left over after making *lapin à la moutarde*. Dried and cured, they could be sewn together into a furry *plastron*, or chest protector, for one's adopted *filleul*, or godson.

The appeal for *marraines de guerre* was always assumed to have been a spontaneous expression by men at the front who, seeing no end to the war, reached out for a lifeline to the real world. Others suggested it was a cynical initiative by government propagandists to placate increasingly disgruntled *poilus*.

Neither was true. It was a purely commercial proposition, invented by old hands at the game. The proof is in the ads themselves, most of which ask respondents to write "chez Iris."

Agence Iris was one of Paris's longest-established matrimonial agencies. Mostly it placed ads on behalf of hopeful men and women. Replies went to its offices at 22 rue Saint-Augustin, where advertisers rented boxes to receive them. The agency wasn't too fussy about who used its services. It was widely understood by adulterers that a box at Agence Iris simplified a clandestine correspondence. Iris also inserted advertisements and fielded replies on behalf of such "manicurists" as Miss Mohawk, as well as shady doctors offering to cure sexually transmitted diseases.

Regular clients of the agency included Henry Désiré

Landru, a dapper gentleman, always impeccably dressed, with a gleaming bald head and a flowing red beard. He almost always placed the same advertisement: "Widower with two children, aged 43, with comfortable income, serious and moving in good society, desires to meet widow with a view to matrimony." Nobody inquired why he needed three boxes to handle the replies—until they found that he inserted the same advertisement under ninety different names and responded to approaches from 283 women, 10 of whom were never seen again.

Overstretched in wartime, the police gave a low profile to missing persons, particularly as single women often moved without notice. A shortage of men had opened the market for female transport workers, shop assistants, and nurses. Once Landru's activities were uncovered, they found that he checked each woman in person before deciding whether or not to murder them. Some he discarded. Many he seduced. One has to admire his systematic approach, not to mention his stamina. A typical schedule for May 19, 1915, read:

9.30. Cigarette kiosk Gare de Lyon. Mlle. Lydie.
10.30. Café Place St. Georges, Mme. Ho.——
11.30. Metro Laundry. Mme. Le C——
14.30. Concorde North-South. Mme. Le ——

15.30. Tour St. Jacques. Mme. Du——
17.30. Mme. Va.——
20.15. Saint Lazare. Mme. Le ——

Apparently just as tireless in the bedroom, Landru passed his evenings with a succession of these women in one of the seven city and four suburban apartments he rented under aliases. If they asked about his business, he claimed he'd been in aviation before the Germans seized his factories. If they pressed, he would describe his product, a variation on the whaling harpoon meant to skewer fighter planes in midair. (The French air force actually experimented with such a weapon but found it too heavy.)

Sometimes Landru's conquests were simply romantic, but the ten women he murdered, all widows, had money and were prepared to sign it over to him as a *dot*, or dowry, in return for a respectable marriage. Once he had their cash, he invited them for a weekend in his country house, killed and dismembered them, and cremated them in the kitchen stove. The bodies were never found, but a simple error of thrift caught him out. Knowing his companions would not be coming back, he bought return rail tickets for himself but only one-way for them.

*T*he *marraines de guerre* were Agence Iris's greatest success. By the end of the war, it had handled between 200,000 and 300,000 such advertisements. "*Marraines* came in many forms," wrote historian Alastair Horne. "Sometimes frightened soldiers would be prompted into action by fear more of their *marraine*'s contempt than of their lieutenant's revolver. For the majority, the *marraine* was simply an unseen, unknown Beatrice who wrote her soldier beautiful letters telling him to be brave and die well; the happy minority sometimes also found her willing to share her bed with him on leave."

This underestimates the appeal to both men and women of a practical application of the truism "All's fair in love and war." Not only did women suffer just as much from *cafard* as men: there was a well-established tradition of casual sex in wartime, the so-called *repos du guerrier*, or warrior's rest. In *Also Sprach Zarathustra*, Friedrich Nietzsche wrote, "Man is made for war, woman is made for the warrior's repose, and the rest is madness."

Wealthy women even adopted exotic godsons as accessories. One Australian visitor to the Bois de Boulogne noted, "It seems to be the fashion to have a black *filleul*, and one princess was strolling along with her husband and a coal black negro of the French Colonial Army."

The theater wasn't slow to pick up on the phenomenon. In *La Marraine de l'Escouade* (The Godmother of the Squad), the heroine dresses as a boy to reach the front and find her fiancé, but the big success was *La Marraine des Poilus* in October 1916, in which Lily Grey, alias Lillian Isaacs, stopped the show with her version of, inevitably, "Tipperary." Some true stories of *marraines* read like fiction. One sergeant accumulated forty-four godmothers. When he found he couldn't enjoy them all during a single leave, he deserted to devote himself to their gratification.

The satirical magazines were, as always, frank about what was really going on. In *La Baïonnette*, a soldier describes taking his *pote* to meet his *marraine de guerre*. "As soon as I said, 'This man is my mate,' she immediately, out of consideration for him, introduced him to her maid." *La Vie Parisienne*, where many of the ads appeared, showed a young officer in the boudoir of a pink-cheeked, obviously satisfied woman. "Well, godson," she says, "you're not shy! You got to know my bed very quickly." He replies, "It's my business, dear godmother. I'm liaison officer for the troops who feel out the lay of the land."

Occasionally a misstep took place. A postcard circulated showing a woman opening a drawer on her bedside

Jadis, souvent gentille demoiselle
Trouvait dans son tiroir.. Polichinelle !
Au lieu de cela elle ne trouve plus
Dans son tiroir, qu'un petit poilu !

table, revealing, to her delight, a little soldier holding out his arms. The rhyme, roughly translated, says, "In the past, a woman opening her drawer was likely to find a little *Polichinelle*"—Punchinella, from Punch and Judy—"but today it's more likely to be a *poilu*." A "Punchinella in the drawer" corresponded to the British "bun in the oven," meaning, to be pregnant. Fortunately, help was at hand. The same magazines that ran ads for the *marraines de guerre* also carried notices placed by *faiseuses des anges*—angel makers, or abortionists, so called because they sent unwanted babies straight to heaven.

❊ · 29 · ❊

Blighty

The narrow ways of English folk
Are not for such as we;
They bear the long accustomed yoke
Of staid conservancy.

ANDREW BARTON "BANJO" PATERSON,

"The Old Australian Ways," 1902

The winter of 1917 was no time to be in London. But Archie had nothing to say in the matter. On February 10, after a month in hospital at Etaples, he was sent back to England with a warrant for admission to the military hospital at Lakenham, outside Norwich.

When the boat docked in Folkestone, he took the train to London. From Waterloo Station, he needed to cross the city to Liverpool Street Station for the hundred-mile trip to Norwich. But what visitor from the far side of the world could resist the temptation to spend at least an evening in the city regarded by Anglo-Saxons as the heart of civilization?

This, after all, was Blighty, the homeland that Tommies imbued with an almost mystical air of perfection. From the Afghan word *bilāyatī*, meaning "home," Blighty was used by Indians and British soldiers posted to India as an all-purpose adjective for anything English.

Early in the war, the word assumed all the longing of nostalgia. "Blighty leave" was time spent on the other side of the Channel. A "Blighty wound" was one that got you discharged. It turns up in such popular songs as "There's a Ship That's Bound for Blighty," "We Wish We Were in Blighty," and in particular, "Take Me Back to Dear Old Blighty," which articulated the homesickness of the Tommy in the trenches.

> *Take me back to dear old Blighty!*
> *Put me on the train for London town!*
> *Take me over there,*
> *Drop me anywhere,*
> *Liverpool, Leeds, or Birmingham, well, I don't care!*

No other country had Britain's idealized concept of a national homeland. A doughboy could sing "Swanee, how I love ya, how I love ya" without implying any

The Home Guard

superiority to another's "little gray home in the west." Australians loyally sang along with their British and American comrades, as enthusiastic for Tipperary or Tralee or Texas as if they'd actually been there.

Among themselves, Australians didn't sing about places but people, and in particular figures from the country's criminal past: "The Wild Colonial Boy," "Waltzing Matilda," and a rogues' gallery of bushrangers, as highwaymen were called, in particular Ben Hall and the folk hero Ned Kelly. It wasn't until the postwar rise of nationalism that they would start singing about "the track winding back to an old familiar shack along the road to Gundagai."

In London, Archie reported to AIF headquarters in Horseferry Road. Any serviceman who failed to do so risked being listed absent without leave and hunted down by the feared and despised military police or provosts. The Horseferry Road complex, a former Methodist training college on a dingy street near the Thames, was branded "a slum" by the official Australian war historian, and worse by the men who used it. But Archie could collect his pay there, eat (free) at the noisy, crowded Anzac buffet restaurant, funded by the Australian Natives Association, or pay for a quieter dinner at the army-run Australian Soldiers Club. After that, they'd find him a bed in one of the bleak hostels maintained for troops in transit. In between, he would have dodged the prostitutes, amateur and professional, who haunted the area, on the lookout for well-paid and free-spending Aussies.

Next day, he probably drew a new uniform. As fleas

and lice were an occupational hazard anywhere troops gathered, soldiers never missed an opportunity, in the days before dry cleaning, to boil their clothes or, better still, turn them in for a new set. Archie also received a warrant for the train journey to Norwich. This would have brought him in contact with the AIF's notorious bureaucracy. It so enraged one anonymous serviceman that he composed a song that, in various degrees of profanity and bile, was still being sung as recently as the Vietnam War.

He was stranded alone in London, and strode
To Army Headquarters in Horseferry Road,
And there met a poofter Lance Corporal, who said
"You've got blood on your tunic, you've mud on
      your head;
You look so disgraceful that people will laugh,"
Said the cold-footed bastard from the Horseferry
      staff.
The digger jumped up with a murderous glance;
Said "Fuck you. I just came from the trenches in
      France
Where fighting was plenty and cunt was for few
And brave men are dying for mongrels like you."

Over the years, the song acquired numerous additions, including one with a happy ending.

Well, the question soon came to the ears of Lord Gort
Who gave the whole matter a good deal of thought;
He awarded that digger a VC with bars
For giving that Corporal a kick up the arse.

Australians were everywhere in London. Neither their good nature nor their bombast could be ignored. It was a standing joke that every digger, true to his nickname, claimed to own a gold mine back home, or thousands of acres teeming with cattle, sheep, or, to believe the more outrageous liars, kangaroos. Both the Aussies' thirst for beer and their belligerence when drunk were legendary, but most irritating to the British high command was their contempt for authority.

Some officers adjusted better than others. General William Birdwood, born in India of British parents, commanded the Australians at Gallipoli, and earned their respect for his personal courage, if not for the orders imposed on him by London. Though Anzacs referred to him as "Birdy," sometimes within his hearing, he accepted it as the price of their respect and cooperation. Supreme Allied Commander Douglas Haig believed his methods undermined discipline. "Instead of facing the problem," he wrote, "he had gone in for saying everything is perfect, and making himself as popular as possible."

A story went round of Birdwood chatting with a friend in the street when an Australian soldier passed without saluting.

"Aren't you going to call him back and tear him off a strip?" asked the friend.

"And be abused by one of my own men in the middle of the Strand?" Birdwood said mildly. "Why would I want that?"

*U*nlike Paris, which did its best to deny the reality of war, London embraced it with the fanaticism of a monk for his hair shirt. Ordinary life was put aside. Magazines, newspapers, and books dwindled in size as paper was rationed. Voice radio, poised to become a mass medium, was taken over by the armed forces, to be used exclusively by the military, particularly on ships at sea.

Before the war, moralists would have protested the suggestiveness of Arthur Wimperis's lyrics for the recruiting song "I'll Make a Man of You." But nobody objected when they were sung in the cause of keeping up the number of volunteers.

> *On Sunday I walk out with a Soldier,*
> *On Monday I'm taken by a Tar,*
> *On Tuesday I'm out with a baby Boy Scout,*
> *On Wednesday a Hussar;*
> *On Thursday a gang oot wi' a Scottie,*
> *On Friday, the Captain of the crew;*
> *But on Saturday I'm willing, if you'll only take the*
> *shilling,*
> *To make a man of any one of you.*

Crude propaganda such as Harold Begbie's poem *Fall-In* took a different line, playing on the very British concern for What People Will Say.

> *What will you lack, sonny, what will you lack*
> *When the girls line up the street,*
> *Shouting their love to the lads come back*
> *From the foe they rushed to beat?*
> *Will you send a strangled cheer to the sky*
> *And grin till your cheeks are red?*
> *But what will you lack when your mates go by*
> *With a girl who cuts you dead?*

Unrelenting peer pressure urged men of draft age to "take the king's shilling" and enlist. Any young man not in uniform risked being handed a white feather, the symbol of cowardice. Women approaching him in the street would smile and show every sign of interest— then, as they got closer, register repugnance at his civilian clothes.

France had self-appointed patriots too, but didn't take them seriously. One cartoon showed the speaker at a woman's group announcing melodramatically, "I swear I will never marry any man who returns from the trenches alive!" Nor were their critics afraid to point out that talk was cheap: the women encouraging men to fight would never have to face a bullet themselves.

Any Briton brave enough to plead conscientious objections to the war faced the risk of elaborate cruelty, even death, certainly privation, imprisonment, hard labor. Even so, sixteen thousand applied for exemption, although few achieved it. One absolutist who refused to contribute to the war in any way, even by helping the injured, was forced into uniform and taken to the trenches under guard. He promptly stripped off the battle dress and walked back behind the lines naked.

Some people made their point with less agony. The writer Lytton Strachey was so frail he would never have

been called up, but he chose to plead conscientious ob-
jection as a way of protesting the war. Tall and gan-
gling, with a long beard and a fussy, effeminate manner,
he turned the hearing into a farce. Complaining of the
hardness of the courtroom benches, he produced an air
cushion, which he noisily inflated. When the chairman
of the panel asked the standard question, "What would
you do if you saw a German soldier about to violate your
sister?" Strachey replied in his fluting falsetto, "I would
try to interpose my body between them."

*B*y 1917, the war was costing Britain, in today's
terms, twenty million pounds an hour, three
billion pounds a week. Through sheer willpower, the
country had wrenched itself from a civilian to a military economy. Women worked in factories and took
over large parts of the public services. Pots, pans, and
the railings around parks and churches were melted
down for weapons. All food was severely rationed, not
to mention beer, tobacco, coffee, and tea. Such was the
need for acetone, a component of the explosive cordite,
that much of the grain harvest was allocated to its fer-
mentation. Starvation was averted only when Chaim
Weizmann discovered how to make it from chestnuts.

Every child in the British Isles was instantly ordered to gather them.

In February 1917, while Archie was in London, revolution ended the rule of the czars. That an ancient monarchy could be toppled overnight, and by the very people it ruled, shocked royalty everywhere, particularly since many crowned heads were cousins, descended from the remarkably fecund Victoria and Albert. The abdication of Nicholas II made his cousin, George V of England, who resembled him enough to be his brother, realize no throne was safe. He renounced the family name of Saxe-Coburg-Gotha, replacing it with Windsor, after the favorite castle of Queen Victoria. His subjects welcomed the gesture. *Punch* published a cartoon of his majesty, in ermine robes, using a yard broom to sweep everything German from Britain.

Anti-Teutonic sentiment, already high, hardened as Gotha bombers flying from bases in occupied Belgium dropped high explosives on the Channel ports and, occasionally, London. The RAF's underpowered fighters had made easy meat of lumbering low-flying zeppelins but couldn't climb fast or far enough to attack the Gothas. All the same, many more people died than should have, because, instead of hiding, they ran out to see the show. The government responded by imposing a blackout in towns or cities within bombing range. Street lighting and illuminated signs disappeared. Heavy curtains covered every window. London reverted to the gloom of Victorian times, the funereal city evoked by Dickens in *Bleak House*.

> *Smoke lowering down from chimney-pots, making a soft black drizzle, with flakes of soot in it as big as full-grown snowflakes—gone into mourning, one might imagine, for the death of the sun. Dogs, undistinguishable in mire. Horses, scarcely better; splashed to their very blinkers. Foot passengers, jostling one another's umbrellas in a general infection of ill temper, and losing their foot-hold at street-corners, where tens of thousands of other foot passengers have been slipping and sliding since the day broke (if this day ever broke), adding new deposits to the crust upon crust of mud, sticking at those points tenaciously to the pavement, and accumulating at compound interest.*

After the sunny calm of Sydney, its wide empty streets and limitless food, London was disorienting. The average Australian arriving in 1917 was, as one historian wrote, "astounded by the scale and magnificence of even

A London bus conductress

a blacked-out capital, and inexpert in dealing with its more opportunistic inhabitants. Besides their awe at historic buildings they had only ever heard of, they gaped at its traffic-clogged streets, its vastness, the modernity of escalators and the wonders of the Underground."

I see Archie as part of that crowd. That's him waiting at the bus stop next to Piccadilly Circus, a tall young man, face as dreamy under the flat cap as it had been in his wedding photograph, hands shoved in the pockets of his army greatcoat, a sausage-shaped canvas kitbag beside him. As the bus arrives, he climbs onto the open back platform, wincing from the pain in his legs. The conductor, a pretty girl, grabs his bag and hauls him aboard.

"Cummon, Aussie! Ups a daisy!"

Her familiarity embarrasses him. He still isn't comfortable speaking to women, least of all one as self-assured as this girl, effortlessly doing a man's job. Once she's clipped his ticket (a flake of card falling to join the confetti littering the platform), he hauls his bag up the spiral stairs to the open upper deck. Most passengers prefer to stay below, inside, but a few huddle up here, sufficiently interested, like him, in the sights of London not to mind the cold.

Knowing that, one day, he'll be asked, "What's London *really* like?" he watches, dutifully, taking note: the mixture of automobiles and horse-drawn wagons in the streets below; the gray granite frontages of the City, as London's financial center is known; the occasional church, discreet but proud and superior in that eighteenth-century way Australia will never achieve. It is, he decides tentatively, looking up into the overcast, something to do with the light.

"Liverpool Street. Liverpool Street Station."

A minute later, he's on the curb, staring up at a

block-long berg of ash-gray brick. It dwarfs the people surging through its wide doors and the motor cabs that clatter up the incline to the main entrance. Not just a railway station, the complex, as befits the station serving the City, houses a hotel, shops, offices, and the largest Masonic temple in Britain. Shouldering his bag, he trudges up the slope. In May, a thousand-pound bomb from a Gotha G.V will crash through the glass roof of the main concourse and kill 162 people. Archie has no conception of such disasters, any more than millions of other people involved in this war, except that, of course, they will never happen to him.

He is mostly aware of himself—his cold, his hunger, his loneliness. Any fears are not of bullet, bomb, or bayonet but of childish things—getting lost, looking foolish, being found out. Tears come to his eyes. Though he believed, on so gratefully leaving Australia, that he would never feel such an emotion again, he wishes he were back home.

30

Dancing Between the Flames

I beached upon—imagine!—incredible Floridas
Where panthers with the skins of men
In flowers glide. Where rainbow bridles,
Horizon-wide, rein the ocean's pearly herds.
ARTHUR RIMBAUD, "The Drunken Boat"

No matter how catastrophic the reverses at the front, and how ominous the news that Russia, now ruled by the Communists, was negotiating a separate peace, Paris plugged its ears and covered its eyes. "The worse the war is, the more depraved the civilians become," novelist Louis-Ferdinand Céline grumbled in *Journey to the End of the Night*. "Women seem to have a fire in their ass. In time of war, in-

L'Assiette
au
Beurre

Nº 152. — 27 Février 1904.

40 CENTIMES

RASTAQUOUÈRES

EXTES DE

PAUL PIALLURIAU

a...
of t...
bars.
theatre...

stead of dancing in the lobby, we dance in the cellar."

Shifty people of every stripe gravitated to the rich pickings of a city at war. Among them were numerous *rastaquouères*: *rastas* for short, from the Spanish *rastacuero*, meaning social climber or nouveau riche. *Rastaquouère* became an all-purpose label for any suave but untrustworthy foreigner, the "oily Levantine," typically from the eastern Mediterranean or Latin America, with enough money to live well and the manners to move in society. They were, almost by definition, crooked. Many were gamblers. Some dealt in drugs. Others worked as pimps or gigolos. Even before the war, they'd excited suspicion. The anarchist review *L'Assiette au Beurre* devoted an entire issue to them. The cover showed a dark-skinned hand, with a diamond ring on every finger, thrusting a knife through a queen of hearts.

Rastas clustered around the Opéra, where, in a phrase of Pierre Darmon, "a varied fauna had taken over the cafés and bars." The security services kept an eye on these places. Reports filed by their spies are snapshots of a hermetic and fevered world. "Seen at Ciro's, in a ultrafantastic uniform, young R——, son of a judge he court of appeal and a regular in the fashionable Also George M——, secretary general of the Michel." A black market flourished wherever the rich hung out, such as the bar at Maxim's restaurant on rue Royale. "At Maxim's, a fat man with the ribbon of the Légion d'Honneur explained to a couple of regulars how he got cigarettes via his member of parliament."

Foreign journalists congregated at the Café Napolitain on rue de Caumartin, along with artists and the better class of prostitute. In the basement oyster bar of the Cintra on Place Edouard VII, inspectors noted "pederasts both civilian and military, some of them in make-up, some young men who, astonishingly, had escaped the draft, and a number of strangers with the air of *rastas*." The latter were probably there to buy or sell cocaine, or to trade in jewelry, often stolen.

Though it limited the number of foreigners accepted into the army, the French were more welcoming to aviators, who were harder to find and died even more quickly than infantrymen. American volunteers formed the Lafayette Flying Corps, whose fliers were frequently seen around the boulevards, wearing high-laced leather boots, riding breeches, smart jackets with lots of braid, and sometimes a leather flying helmet.

Among them was William Wellman Jr. of Brookline, Massachusetts. He volunteered to drive an ambulance, switched to the Foreign Legion, then, like Eugene Bullard, transferred to the Lafayette Flying Corps, achieved three confirmed "kills" and five probables, earned the Croix de Guerre, but was himself shot down. This left "Wild Bill" with a lifelong limp, which, he claimed, increased his attractiveness to women. He later married one of Busby Berkeley's showgirls and directed such movies as *Wings*, *Roxie Hart*, and *Battleground*.

Real aviators, such as Wellman and the African American Eugene Bullard, drank at the Rotonde in Montparnasse, where Bullard became friendly with the painter Moise Kisling, or at Chez le Père Lebas on rue Caumartin, where he went with another pilot, Jean Navarre. The first time Navarre took Bullard there, the regulars fell silent at the sight of his black skin. Someone said to Navarre, "Where did you get that? And what is it? Whatever it is, put it in the toilet and don't forget to pull the chain." Furious, Bullard, who had boxed professionally, prepared to take the bar apart—until Navarre reassured him it was just the "hazing" dished out to all new arrivals.

Such men as Wellman and Bullard turned *la mode d'aviateur* into a fashion statement. In turn, it became a gay fad, like the uniform Poiret designed for Misia Sert's ambulance service. Police scouting the métro station in front of the Opéra reported "two 'aviators' in make-up, wearing outrageously tight trousers, which roused the hostility of passersby and some *poilus*." At the American

"Powdered type, difficult to categorize."

cocktail bar in the Grand Hotel on rue Auber, they spotted more of them, "dressed in fantastic uniforms, with no badges indicating their unit, and wearing their *kepis* tilted on the back of their heads, like jockeys. These absurdities were regarded with disapproval by the public."

Any dedicated follower of fashion who found uniforms too butch could opt for the *flâneur* or *boulevardier* style: a flannel jacket with a nipped-in waist, slim-cut striped trousers, shoes with canvas spats, the whole topped off with a jaunty felt hat, a cane, and, often, a monocle. As this look flattered both men and women, even the police couldn't tell them apart. At the Chatham on rue Danou and the nearby Tipperary bar, the clientele consisted of "officers, straights and shady characters, *rastas*, and some powdered types, difficult to categorize."

A few doors from the Chatham was Harry's New York Bar, where the Bloody Mary was invented; George Gershwin would one day compose *Rhapsody in Blue* in the basement. An American jockey, Tod Sloan, opened Harry's in 1911. Believing Paris needed a place where New Yorkers could feel at home, he bought a Manhattan bar and shipped its fixtures and furnishings to France. Everyone on the staff spoke English, a fact promoted in its advertising, which included a phonetic rendering of the address as "Sank Roo Da Noo," making it easy for thirsty tourists to ask directions.

Harry's barman, Jimmie Charters, would later serve "behind the stick" at the Dingo Bar in Montparnasse, where Hemingway and Scott Fitzgerald first met. When he published his memoirs, *This Must Be the Place*, Hemingway wrote an introduction, in which he couldn't resist sniping at James Joyce and, in particular, Gertrude Stein, from whose salon he had been barred after a literary argument. "Jimmy served more and better drinks than any legendary woman ever did in her salon," he wrote; "certainly Jimmy gave less and better advice."

31

I Love a Parade!

There is work to be done, to be done
There's a war to be won, to be won
Come, you son of a son of a gun,
Take your stand
Fall in line, yea a bow
Come along, let's go
Hey, leader, strike up the band!

IRA GERSHWIN, "Strike Up the Band"

Cocteau and Picasso returned from Rome not only with Diaghilev's endorsement of their ballet idea but, in Picasso's case, a new love. He'd fallen for one of the impresario's dancers, Olga Khokhlova. She joined him in Paris. At their July 1918 wedding in the grandiose Russian Orthodox church, Cocteau was one of the witnesses.

Olga danced in the first performance of *Parade*,

a charity matinee that began at 3:45 p.m. on May 18, 1917. Although the piece only lasted thirty minutes, Diaghilev's favorite Paris venue, the three-thousand-seat Théâtre du Châtelet on the right bank of the Seine, within sight of Notre Dame, was jammed. Before the war, it had specialized in spectacles, in particular a multimedia production of Jules Verne's *Around the World in Eighty Days*, which ran intermittently for more than two thousand performances and was only mothballed when the Nazis occupied the city in 1940. As a child, Cocteau saw this showcase of theatrical effects. It excited him so much that he ran a temperature. The family thought he was ill. Jean concurred. "I *had* caught something—the red-and-gold disease, theatre-itis." It proved incurable.

During the staging of *Parade*, Cocteau complained that there was insufficient light on stage.

> *"Monsieur Colombier," I said to the chief electrician. "I want the lighting you had for the Vegetable Kingdom in La Biche au Bois."*
>
> *"How old were you then, Monsieur Cocteau?"*
> *"Five."*
> *"The lighting was the same as you have now," he replied. "At that date, the theatre did not possess one quarter of the present equipment."*

*Alas, the gold on the crimson curtain and the
brazier footlights will never again scorch our scepti-
cal childish eyes.*

In December 1915, continuing its tradition of spectacle, the Châtelet staged *Les Exploits d'une Petite
Française*—The Exploits of a Little French Girl—
which, according to the publicity, "had them talking in
the trenches." The story, which echoed, presumably not
by accident, Verne's classic adventure, revolved around
a new explosive invented by a Frenchman living in Australia. Attempts to get the formula across the world to
France are impeded by a German spy, but he is outwit-
ted by the inventor's servant and his resourceful girlfriend. A review of the show suggests what the Châtelet
could achieve when it pulled out the stops. "After some
agreeable ballets, an oil field in flames and an encounter
between a zeppelin and an aeroplane, the little French
girl tips the spy into a vat of molten steel in a German
factory. There's an explosion of horror on stage and of
joy in the theatre."

In expectation of similar, if more intellectual fire-
works, spectators crowded the Châtelet for *Parade*. A
collaboration between three such *avant gardistes* as Cocteau, Satie, and Picasso had already caught the atten-

tion of the Montparnos. According to the buzz round the cafés, Picasso's cubist costumes were astonishing and Satie's music typically quirky. As for Cocteau . . . well, who knew what he would come up with?

The *loges*, or private boxes, were taken by Diaghilev's unfailing supporters and financial backers: Etienne and Edith de Beaumont, Misia Sert, and the Princess de Polignac, all with their entourages. But the audience was genuinely international. Young American writer e. e. cummings, absent without leave from his ambulance unit, had scrounged a seat. Picasso's involvement guaranteed a Spanish contingent, including piano virtuoso Ricardo Vines and painter Juan Gris. Diaghilev, as well as inviting some Russian soldiers on leave, shrewdly sent tickets to tastemakers from Montparnasse and Montmartre. They included Guillaume Apollinaire, who'd written the program notes even though his head was still bandaged from a war wound, and the young composers George Auric and Francis Poulenc, barely out of their teens but already disciples of Satie.

The irascible Satie made no secret of his anger at Cocteau's additions to his score, in particular mechanical sounds: typewriting, Morse code, a dynamo, sirens, a locomotive, an airplane, and a passage played by banging on milk bottles filled to different levels with water.

Asked to describe his music, he said acidly, "I composed a background to certain noises that Cocteau says he needed to point up his characters." At rehearsals, the orchestra struggled to understand his meticulous notation and initially treated it as dance music. When he insisted on precision, a flautist said, "Monsieur Satie, you must think I'm stupid." Satie said mildly, 'I don't think you're stupid—but I could be wrong." Cocteau had to call on another member of Misia Sert's circle, the composer Maurice Ravel, to quell the revolt.

Almost as attractive to the audience as the promise of novelty was the sense that *Parade* itself and one's presence at the premiere was a way of defying the war. "The holocaust was now in its third year," wrote Cocteau's biographer Francis Steegmuller. "Russia had defaulted. Allied morale was low. The first half of May was a period of almost incredible slaughter on the western front; each day thousands of Frenchmen and their allies perished in seemingly futile attacks against German lines along the River Aisne, and among the French troops there were mutinies against the incessant commands to commit almost certain suicide by going over the top in the face of machine-gun fire."

Attendance at *Parade* was not only fashionable but a gesture of support for the city's embattled theatrical managements and performers. Wartime Paris was no place for first-nighters. Buses and the métro halted at 10:00 p.m. With the gas shortage, taxis had almost disappeared. Electricity for light and heating was rationed, and street lighting dimmed. Worse, a new ordinance cut to four the number of nights on which a theater could open; hence the afternoon premiere of *Parade*. Venues were also required to close at 11:00 p.m. Those that didn't close their doors altogether shut off their upper circles and the *promenoirs* where so much socializing took place.

With Gotha attacks a regular event, cinemas and theaters were given the option, providing they displayed a notice in the foyer, of halting or continuing performances during a raid. Most continued. Hector Brewer, a lieutenant in the AIF, was in Paris during March 1918, and experienced an air raid at the Folies Bergère.

The Huns raided the city whilst we were in the music hall and dropped a bomb about one block away. The girls and women were very frightened and some of the men too and it looked as if they would start a panic but some French officers saved the situation by asking the orchestra to continue playing and got everybody to clap their hands and cheer and do anything to keep

*the minds of the people away from the danger which
after all was not very great.*

*Great credit is due to these French officers for their
timely and excellent advice. Had a panic ensued,
numbers of people must have been killed in trying to
get out. A number of soldiers kept a large section of
the crowd busy by dancing and singing. It was not
long before the All Clear was sounded by the police
going round the city in a car blowing a horn and
everybody was soon quite happy and smiling again.*

One venue where everyone expected the management to honor the tradition of "The show must go on" was the Grand Guignol, which staged sadistic melodramas of torture, mutilation, and murder. However, the siren halted even its performances. The problem wasn't audiences but actresses. Women used to miming having their eyes gouged out with a hat pin or their face pressed to a red hot stove could imagine all too well the effect of a bomb landing in the stalls and headed straight for the cellar at the first wail of a siren.

From the moment the curtain went up on *Parade*, it was clear that this was just what the doctor ordered for the floundering theater. Picasso's backcloth overflowed with elements direct from the fun fair. As a girl in a tutu balances on a winged white horse, a group of carnies watch without much interest. At the rear, a monkey climbs a ladder. In the foreground, a whippet dozes. In his program notes, Apollinaire, almost in passing, described the conception as "a sort of surrealism"—not fantasy, but the real world twisted at a slightly different angle. In 1917, André Breton was still working in the neurological ward of a hospital in Nantes and Louis Aragon was studying medicine, but once they began formulating their variations and refinements of dada, Breton remembered Apollinaire's coining the word "surrealism" and adopted it as the name of his creation.

The dancing, choreographed by Léonide Massine, who had replaced Nijinsky in Diaghilev's bed, affronted balletomanes even more than the score enraged musicians. It incorporated ragtime, the cakewalk, and other dances previously seen only in American minstrel shows. James Reese Europe had popularized—he said "invented"—the particularly scandalous one-step, calling it "the national dance of the Negro." Francis Poulenc shared the general shock of seeing it on a respectable stage. "For the first time, music hall was in-

vading art-with-a-Capital-A. A one-step is danced in
Parade! When *that* began, the audience let loose with
boos and applause."

In designing his cubist costumes for the two "managers," or barkers, Picasso adapted the appearance of
sandwich men who patrolled the streets, draped front
and rear in panels promoting cut-price suits or cheap
eats. He exaggerated these into cardboard towers
eleven feet tall, plastered with advertising, just as he and
Braque had pasted scraps of posters and newspaper into
their canvases. Half man, half billboard, the managers
were physical manifestations of a frenzy to promote. "As
they stumped about the stage," wrote English surreal-
ist Roland Penrose, "they complained to each other in
their formidable language that the crowd was mistaking
the preliminary parade for the real show, for which no
one had turned up. Finally their fruitless efforts brought
them to a state of exhaustion and they collapsed on the
stage, where they were found by the actors, who in turn
also failed to entice an imaginary crowd inside."

The moment the piece ended, the huge theater
erupted with cheers and catcalls. Cocteau, with cus-
tomary exaggeration, wrote, "I have heard the cries of
a bayonet charge in Flanders, but it was nothing compared to what happened that night at the Châtelet The-

atre." Supposedly a group of women shouted *"Boches!"* They spotted Cocteau crossing the stalls through the milling crowd, yelled "There's one of them," and tried to skewer him with hat pins. Apollinaire with his ample bulk and bandaged head saved him. "If I'd known it was going to be this silly," said a spectator, "I'd have brought the kids."

After the performance, music critic Jean Poueigh shook Satie's hand—only to savage the composer in his review the next day, accusing him of lacking invention, wit, and professional skill. Despite his long beard and playful eccentricities, which included eating only foods that were white and always wearing identical gray suits, Satie, in the words of Nina Hamnett, "had a most malicious tongue and a diabolical face." He sent Poueigh a series of postcards, beginning with *"Monsieur et cher ami—vous êtes un cul, un cul sans musique! Offrez-moi jamais de nouveau votre main sale."* (Sir and dear friend— you are an asshole, an asshole without music! Never again offer me your dirty hand.) The abuse escalated to "Monsieur Fuckface Poueigh, Famous Pumpkin and Composer for Nitwits. Lousy asshole, this is from where I shit on you with all my strength."

Poueigh brought a criminal case for defamation, claiming the cards might have been read by mail sort-ers and his concierge, thus damaging his reputation. At the trial, Cocteau brandished his cane at Poueigh's lawyer. Satie was sentenced to a hundred-franc fine, a thousand francs in damages to Poueigh, and eight days in jail. Press reports infuriated him even more with their patronizing remarks about "the old artist" who "had written what he called 'the music.' " The fine and prison term were finally set aside, but not without a strenuous and protracted fight.

Parade achieved Cocteau's aim in making a scandal to rival *The Rite of Spring*. He was even more content when stories got around that sensation seekers with access to a private box liked to have sex while they watched the show. Some Paris theaters already offered *loges* with lockable doors for patrons who enjoyed this piquant combination of seclusion and exhibitionism, but to experience those pleasures in as vast a venue as the Châtelet was something new. One gossip wrote of "madness in the *loges*. To make love during *Parade* was the last word. That harsh lighting, that crude music with no flourishes, went straight to the heart"—or more likely the groin. It really was the hottest ticket in town.

· 32 · ❦

Every Night Something Awful

An army marches on its stomach.

NAPOLEON I

The war began in 1914 as a clash between concepts noble enough to be capitalized: Pride, Patriotism, Glory. By 1917, it had degenerated, at least as far as the average Briton was concerned, into a crisis about something much more prosaic—bread.

As his train carried him under lowering clouds across a rainy eastern England, Archie, a countryman at heart, would have understood what he saw in the fields on either side of the line. There was nothing green. Everywhere was fresh-turned earth. War or no war, fields had to be tilled and crops planted.

The 1916 wheat harvest had been poor worldwide. For a century, Britain had imported most of its grain, but in early 1917 Canada and the United States had little surplus to sell. The British could buy from Australia, India, and Argentina, but that meant longer voyages, higher prices, and more risk of attack by German submarines. Hoping to head off a catastrophic food shortage, the army in March 1917 began releasing troops to help with the plowing.

At the same time, they pushed the already overstretched economy to produce more grain and vegetables. Anzacs in England who knew agriculture recognized this as "too little too late." One wrote home, "They are making great efforts to organize the production of the country & orders came through to the Parish Council to cultivate every inch of ground they had to spare for potatoes etc. & the millers have got to put at least 5 percent of oats or barley crush in their flour. British people generally wake up a year or two after they ought to."

In France, food shortages were even more acute because so much of the country was in German hands. The army had commandeered almost all farm horses. In the fields, it was quite usual, with all the fit men at war, to see teams of women yoked to a plow or harrow, dragging it across the fields. Jean Cocteau, as his introduction to the long poem *Le Cap de Bonne-Espérance* (Cape of Good Hope), reproduced without comment the report of a court-martial that took place at the end of 1916.

> *The accused is a forty-three-year-old man, serious and sad. Accused of desertion, he was brought before the 2nd Council of War for the Paris region, presided over by M. Colonel Chartier.*
>
> *The President began by asking "Why did you desert?"*
>
> *The Accused: "I asked for leave but it was refused. Even so, I needed to go to my farm at Stains, near St. Denis. I had potatoes to lift, and they couldn't wait. When I arrived, I went straight to work on the farm. Once I'd lifted the potatoes, I returned right away. I don't believe I was a deserter."*
>
> *The President: "You seem to forget we are at war. Leaving your post to harvest potatoes can't be tolerated. You can't be serious."*
>
> *The Accused: "All the same, I had to lift my potatoes."*

In Berlin, Moscow, Paris, and London, the leaders of the rival powers bickered about what to do next. Both

Kaiser Wilhelm and Czar Nicholas were ditherers with schoolboy notions of politics and economics. The minutes of these meetings show them blustering, cringing, and even weeping as they argue the course of the war. Almost always, they defer in desperation to their military and naval commanders, who are adamant that victory is in sight if they just escalate the violence.

In the end, it came down to submarines. Germany pondered: if it ordered its submarines to attack vessels of all nations bringing cargo to Britain, would the Allies sue for peace before so many American ships were sunk that the United States was forced into the war? As Archie headed across East Anglia, the kaiser finally accepted the assurances of the military and naval hierarchy that unrestricted submarine warfare would starve Britain into surrender within five months. In January, the Wilhelmstrasse announced that, from February 1, ships carrying food or military supplies for the Allies, no matter what flag they flew, risked being sunk. Germany had literally bet the farm.

Among the men released to work on the land was Ellis Evans, better known for his poems in the Welsh language as Hedd Wyn. Evans spent part of his leave on the family's sheep farm writing *Yr Arwr* (The Hero) as his entry to the National Eisteddfod, the Welsh literary festival. "He came back for fourteen days' leave and wrote *Yr Arwr* on the table by the fire," said his nephew, Gerald Williams. "As it was such a wet year, he stayed for another seven days. This extra seven days made him a deserter. So the military police came to fetch him from the hayfield and took him to the jail at Blaenau. From there, he travelled to the war in Belgium."

At the festival on September 6, *Yr Arwr* was unanimously awarded first prize. Traditionally, the winner is called from the audience three times, with a fanfare of trumpets, to take his place in the thronelike bardic chair. To the embarrassment of the judges and guests, who included the prime minister, David Lloyd George, they only then learned that Evans had died on July 31 at Passchendaele. His empty chair was draped in black, and the festival of that year was known ever after as Eisteddfod y Gadair Ddu: the Eisteddfod of the Black Chair.

In early 1917, Britain didn't lack black chairs. Almost every family had lost someone. In some cases, every son was killed, and often the father also. The wounded were piling up. Hospital ships from Etaples now landed at night: better the public didn't see the numbers of injured and dead. With London hospitals full, casualties spilled into the countryside. Those who could walk were sent to the emptier counties of East Anglia—Suffolk and

Railway carriage adapted to carry wounded

Norfolk. Once they recovered, the army shipped them to Codford or Hurdcott on Salisbury Plain to get back in shape before being returned to France.

Archie's train carried scores of men with thickly bandaged limbs or hobbling on crutches. Some had faces ripped by shrapnel; Norwich was a center for the infant craft of reconstructive surgery. Others, wheezing from the effect of gas, were expected to benefit from the fresh, chill winds off the North Sea. Everything had an air of "make-do and mend." Country railway stations became mini-clinics where patients were stabilized and medicated before ambulances, improvised from baker's and milkman's vans, sometimes horse-drawn, carried them along country lanes to one of the region's sixty-two auxiliary hospitals, adapted from schools, insane asylums, mansions, and museums.

Catton Hall, a former stately home, was typical of the hospitals and convalescent centers where Archie spent most of 1917. Patients at Catton were housed in its indoor racquetball court. The family's private museum became a recreation room. In good weather, inmates could sit out under a covered verandah. Small open-sided huts were built for gas victims. Excursions for those who couldn't walk were organized by roping together their wheeled "bath chairs" and towing them in a decorous caravan through the countryside.

Those who could walk were allowed to roam, providing they wore their "hospital blues": a pair of blue flannel trousers, a jacket with pale blue lapels and cuffs, a white shirt, and red tie. Any making it to a village pub in hopes of a drink were turned away. It was illegal to serve alcohol to a man in uniform, even one that resembled pajamas. However, some hospitals provided beer, believing it hastened recovery.

For entertainment, there were tournaments, or "drives," of whist and bridge. Visiting concert parties put on shows. The eight or ten performers of these groups, sometimes dressed in the baggy white suit and conical hat of Pierrot, generally included a pretty young singer or *soubrette*, a male partner for dance duets, an older soprano and a baritone to sing selections from operetta, and a mix of comics, jugglers, and magicians. The troupes competed for catchy names: Pelissier's

Pierrots, including a Charlie Chaplin imitator

Potted Pageant, The Fol-de-Rols, The Lavender Follies, The Quaintesques.

A few performers graduated from concert parties to the professional stage, but most were well-meaning amateurs, particularly those who volunteered to entertain captive audiences like the wounded. Impolite and impatient Australians severely tested their generosity of spirit. Of a group that played the convalescent hospital at Hurdcott, a patient wrote, "I'm hanged if I know why the people stick to the Australians, for they soon let everybody on the stage know if they are not pleasing them." In World War II, when concert parties were again drafted to amuse the troops, critics suggested that ENSA, the initials of the organizing body, the Entertainments National Service Association, stood for "Every Night Something Awful."

Norwich Military Hospital, where Archie went for his surgery, was a flat-faced three-story Victorian redbrick building, topped with an incongruous central clock tower. It had been a school. The headmaster's office was now an operating room. It was there in February 1917 that he underwent surgery. As a nurse dripped chloroform onto a face mask to keep him unconscious, the surgeon made incisions at the top, middle, and bottom of each bulging blue leg vein, fed in a fine wire, tied it to the vein at the three incision points, then pulled out the entire vein. The process would have been repeated on each affected vein, and in both legs.

Without today's pain-killing drugs or antibiotics to fend off infection, Archie's recovery was lengthy and painful. Though he had not been wounded in battle, his suffering was no less acute. But when he hobbled out of the hospital, that had ceased to matter. By March 21, German submarines had sunk seven American merchant ships, an intolerable provocation to the United States. President Wilson summoned Congress and on April 6, 1917, the United States entered the war. On May 18, Congress passed the Selective Service Act, authorizing a draft. It foresaw the U.S. Army of 145,000 men being enlarged to 4 million. It seemed the war would soon be over.

33

The Sammies

Over there, over there,
Send the word, send the word over there
That the Yanks are coming, the Yanks are coming
The drums rum-tumming everywhere.

GEORGE M. COHAN, "Over There"

Lithe as a seal, the woman in the red lycra *maillot* knifed into the shimmering green water and swam toward the picture window at the other end of the pool. Beyond the glass, a lawn trimmed smooth as a putting green sloped up to ground level. It existed only to funnel sunlight into the pool and surrounding restaurant, and appeared indifferent to the fact that, occupying as it did a hundred square meters of Paris's most expensive real estate, each of its impeccably trimmed blades was worth about $10.

"Pretty," I said, nodding toward the swimmer.

Clare looked over the top of her glasses and made a *moue* of disapproval.

" 'Is too slime."

"We say 'slim.' "

Clare was an old friend of Marie-Dominique. I'd known her from my first days in Paris and was almost used to her fractured English. Just after I arrived, she and Marie-Do took me on a Sunday morning promenade down the street market of rue Mouffetard. As we passed a charcuterie, the man sliced a sliver from a large sausage and offered it on the flat of an obviously razor-sharp blade.

Most sausages are pink and marbled with fat. This one was gray, with a structure of concentric rings, like those of a tree. The taste was unexpected also—a faint slipperiness and mustiness.

The charcutier said something. Clare, proud of her store-bought English, started to explain. "Is andouillette. Is make from . . . how you say . . . *tripes*?"

"Guts," Marie-Do said. "Intestines."

"Yes. Zis is 'er," Clare went on. " 'E say—*monsieur le charcutier*—'e say zat he make it *a l'ancienne*. In zer old way."

I nibbled a bit more. What's *was* that odd flavor?

"'E say," Clare continued, "zat 'e put in zer *trou de cul*."

When I looked blank, she scrabbled for a translation, but her vague understanding of the letter *h* got in the way. Since it's seldom pronounced in French, locals tend to scatter it indiscriminately, leaving us to spit out those that don't fit, like seeds in watermelon.

"*Trou de cul, trou de cul*, what *is* zis?" Clare said. Then recollection dawned. "Ha! Yes. I am knowing! *Trou de cul* is zer . . . hasshole!"

As any French person could tell after a glance at Clare's rangy racehorse figure and artfully blonded hair, she came from aristocracy. Better still from my point of view, her father had been in army intelligence during World War II, close to the Free French exiles who ran the underground effort against Hitler from London. As a TV journalist, she'd built on his inside knowledge and contacts to create a formidable *réseau*—a private network of informants and experts. It probably overlapped that of Peter van Diemen, but though each claimed not to be aware of the other's existence, I suspected neither told the truth. Etched deep as tattoos, the habits of espionage are not easily eradicated.

As well as being awesomely well-informed, Clare had entrée to places like this, the *cercle sportif* of the Union Interalliée, the Inter-Allies Club.

Housed in the former mansion of the Baron de Rothschild on rue Faubourg Saint-Honoré, a brief walk away
from the American embassy, and almost next door to the
foreign ministry, the club dated back to 1917. A com-
mittee of wealthy aristos and businessmen decided that
generals of the Allied armies needed a place to socialize
informally and enjoy some foie gras and a decent Bordeaux while deciding the fate of millions. They clubbed
together to acquire the lease and refit it as a private club
for the military elite.

In particular, French and British officers could
mingle here with the Australians and Americans. Perfectly nice chaps, of course, in their own way. But a bit
. . . well, crude. Wore their spurs to the table, poured
their tea into their saucers, blew on the soup—or even
fanned it with their caps. And most troubling of all,
spoke no French.

If the Americans found it hard to communicate
with the French, it was even harder for the French to
make themselves understood. A culture gap yawned.
What the French knew of the United States came from
cheap fiction, visiting vaudeville acts, and the movies.
Just how much they relied on such secondhand sources
became clear when the editor of *La Baïonnette* asked
artist Guy Arnoux to draw a full issue devoted to the

Americans, or, as they were being called, after Uncle Sam, the Sammies—a label Americans hated, and for which they quickly substituted "doughboys."

Perhaps the editor was being mischievous. Or did he not know that Arnoux was an eccentric, with a taste for masquerade? According to Jimmie Charters,

> *His studio was a veritable museum of costumes, knick-knacks, lead soldiers, models of ships, old bottles, telescopes, globes, saddles, and hundreds of other things, a truly remarkable collection. Guy would often wear the costumes, as he liked to dress up, sometimes as a cowboy, or as an officer in the navy, or as a cook, with pots and pans tied from his waist. He attended most of the costume balls of the Quarter, and was always a big success.*

Arnoux's choice of a cover illustration was easy: the heroic image of an American serviceman against the Stars and Stripes. As a model, he chose a marine, a decision followed by most French cartoonists, who found the distinctive high-crowned campaign hat with its four-sided Montana Crease a more arresting silhouette than the duller doughboy cap.

Already nervous about their own rumored fifth

column of German fräuleins, the French were ready to
believe reports that three years of neutrality had made it
possible for a hundred thousand German agents to infil-
trate the United States. On January 11, 1917, two of them

blew up a munitions plant in Kingsland, New Jersey, destroying five hundred shells intended for Russia, killing seventeen people and inflicting an estimated $4 million worth of damage.

Eccentrically, Arnoux linked this to the 1905 and 1906 European tours of Buffalo Bill Cody's Wild West Show, which remained in Paris for many months. In his illustration "The Spy," three cowboys have just hanged a man on a tree, to which is nailed a sign "By Order of Judge Lynch." One says truculently, "100,000 spies, yes—but more than 100,000 trees in the country to hang them from." The cowboy theme continued with a gun-toting cowboy lassoing some Germans, saying, "Germans or cows, it's all the same to me." The Native Americans in Cody's troupe so impressed journalists that they began calling Paris's street gangsters *apaches*, a label that stuck. This was reason enough for Arnoux to draw some of their compatriots in blankets and war bonnets, captioned, "On the Warpath."

For his double-page center spread, however, Arnoux relied on the oldest and soundest example of Franco-American cooperation, the friendship of the Marquis de Lafayette and George Washington. During the War of Independence, the nineteen-year-old aristocrat, drunk on the idea of revolution, had raised a regiment at his own expense and bought a ship to hasten to the aid of the rebels.

Even 150 years later, the mutual affection of France and the United States remained potent. In June, when Pershing arrived in France with his advance guard of two hundred troops of the 16th Infantry Regiment, the public reaction was ecstatic. Delirious Parisians pelted them with flowers. Women jumped out of the crowd to press roses on them. When Pershing visited the Chambre des Deputées, France's parliament, the members stood and cheered.

On July 4, Pershing marched his men through the city to Picpus Cemetery, where Lafayette is buried, surrounded by pits into which the decapitated corpses of hundreds of fellow aristocrats were thrown during the Terror. As Pershing spoke no French, the address was given by an aide, Colonel Charles Stanton. "America," he said, "has joined forces with the Allied Powers, and what we have of blood and treasure are yours. Therefore it is with loving pride that we drape the colors in tribute of respect to this citizen of your great republic. And here and now, in the presence of the illustrious dead, we pledge our hearts and our honor in carrying this war to a successful issue. Lafayette, we are here!"

Behind the official enthusiasm and the patriotic cheers, many Frenchmen were dubious about the Americans. Where had they been for the last three

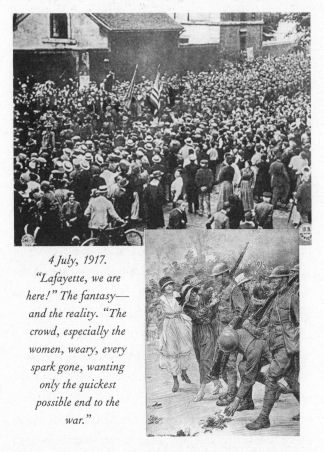

*4 July, 1917.
"Lafayette, we are
here!" The fantasy—
and the reality. "The
crowd, especially the
women, weary, every
spark gone, wanting
only the quickest
possible end to the
war."*

years, while the Allies were fighting the Central powers alone? Significantly, the welcome from Parisians on July 4, in contrast to the ecstasy of a few weeks earlier, was muted. The troops received only sparse applause. In his diary Paul Morand wrote of "the crowd, especially the women, weary, every spark gone, wanting only the quickest possible end to the war."

Some Frenchmen, including many in the military, distrusted the Sammies. Would there be enough of them to turn the tide? Could they fight with the ferocity demanded by the war of attrition to which the French and Dominion forces were now committed? Some in the high command were sure that, at the first shot, these pampered Yanks would cut and run.

When Pershing and his staff got their first look at the enemy, safely, through a telescope in the Saint-Quentin sector, General Pétain listened without expression to Pershing's promises of a million men the first year, increasing to three million in 1918.

"I just hope it is not too late," Pétain said.

He didn't mean "too late to defeat the Germans." With American technology and the sheer weight of numbers, Germany's military annihilation appeared inevitable. But would it ever get that far? Having spent the winter suppressing mutinies, executing their ringleaders, and placating the troops with promises of better treatment and more leave time, Pétain feared his armies were ready to imitate the Russians—simply abandon their weapons and start walking home. If that happened, France and Britain would have no alternative but to follow Russia and negotiate a cease-fire.

After lunch, Clare and I toured the mansion. We wandered through the marble-floored corridors, the formal dining and ballroom, and out into the garden.

Clare paused after a few steps, breathed deep, and said, "Whore's sheet."

I halted. But she was right. The gardener had been spreading manure around the roses.

Seeing my expression, she said, "Is not correct? Whore's sheet?"

I thought of the generals and politicians who dined out here when the weather was warm, and who, after enjoying the *rôti de boeuf poêlé à la Matignon*, strolled along the paths between the perfect flower beds, wrangling in a gentlemanly way over troop allocations and equipment supply while men drowned in the mud of the thaw.

"Horse shit? I couldn't have put it better myself."

34

Things That Go Bump in the Night

*There seems to me to be absolutely no limit to the inanity
and credulity of the human race. Homo sapiens? Homo
idioticus!*

ARTHUR CONAN DOYLE, *The Land of Mist*

Arthur Conan-Doyle, creator of Sherlock Holmes, became increasingly depressed following the death of his wife, Louisa, in 1906 and the wounding of his son, Kingsley, at the Battle of the Somme in 1916. After Kingsley died of his wounds in 1918, along with Doyle's younger brother, Innes, followed by two brothers-in-law and two nephews, he became a believer in psychic phenomena, including fairies, and an aggressive proselytizer. He even wrote a novel in which his alter ego, the irascible but highly rational Professor Challenger, was converted to a belief in the spirit world.

In that novel, *The Land of Mist*, written in 1925, Mr. Miromar, a medium from the unglamorous London suburb of Dalston, receives a message from the Central Intelligence of the universe. It chides mankind for refusing to accept spiritualism, an error for which, he explains, the deaths of the Great War were intended as punishment.

> *Evidence was sent—evidence which made the life after death as clear as the sun in the heavens. It was laughed at by scientists, condemned by the churches, became the butt of the newspapers, and was discarded with contempt. That was the last and greatest blunder of humanity. . . .*
>
> *The thing was now hopeless. It had got beyond all control. Therefore something sterner was needed since Heaven's gift had been disregarded. The blow fell. Ten million young men were laid dead upon the ground. Twice as many were mutilated. That was God's first warning to mankind.*

Further skepticism, warns Miromar, will lead inexorably to the Second Coming.

Europe was not so rational that such ideas would be dismissed with a smirk. Particularly in Catholic cultures like that of France, the church still had influence. Both British Tommies and French *poilus*, mostly uneducated, many of them farmers, were ready to entertain the possibility of divine intervention. God was, after all, On Their Side. That the Germans also insisted *Gott mit uns* didn't trouble them.

From the first battles of the war, tales circulated in France of interventions by Saint Geneviève, the holy guardian of Paris, and acolyte of its patron saint, Saint Denis. In September 1914, Father Sauvêtre, pastor of the church of Saint-Etienne-du-Mont on the site of Montagne–Ste-Geneviève, at the edge of Paris's Latin Quarter, published a booklet, *Saint Geneviève and the German Invasion*, which explained that it wasn't Joffre or Gallieni who saved Paris, but the saint herself.

At almost the same moment, British troops spoke of mysterious manifestations. On August 26, as the Germans poured in through Belgium and overwhelmed the town of Mons, General Horace Smith-Dorrien ordered the forty thousand men of the British Expeditionary Force to defend it as best they could. The effort, finally unsuccessful, cost 7,812 killed, wounded, and missing. The survivors fell back on Le Cateau in a withdrawal that didn't stop until the BEF combined with the French to counter-attack Von Kluck's forces at the Battle of the Marne.

During the days and nights they retreated down endless country roads, exhausted, sleepless, and terrified, British soldiers reported visions. "I had the most amazing hallucinations marching at night," said one young officer, "so I was fast asleep, I think. Everyone was reeling about the road and seeing things. I saw all sorts of things; enormous men walking toward me, and lights and chairs, and things in the road."

Angels on the battlefield

On September 5, Brigadier General John Charteris, the chief intelligence officer, reported that accounts of one vision, the Angel of Mons, were spreading through the ranks. It told "of how the angel of the Lord on the traditional white horse, and clad all in white with flaming sword, faced the advancing Germans at Mons and forbade their further progress." Some men claimed the angel was Joan of Arc, though for her to have intervened on the side of the English, who had burned her at the stake, would have shown truly saintly forbearance.

Tales also circulated of ghostly archers sending clouds of arrows into the German ranks, as phantom bowmen were supposed to have helped win the day for Henry V at Agincourt in 1415. This urban legend at least was easily traced to its source. Welsh author Arthur Machen read of Mons in the Sunday papers. "It was a tale to make the heart sink, almost to deep despair. It told of the British army in full retreat, nay, in headlong, desperate retreat, on Paris. The correspondent rather pictured an army broken to fragments scattered abroad in confusion. It was hardly an army anymore; it was a mob of shattered men." The image inspired him. On September 29, the *London Evening News* published his short story "The Bowman." During a fierce rearguard action, a British soldier recalls seeing the figure of Saint George on the plates in a London restaurant and the motto Adsit Anglis Sanctus Georgius: May Saint George Help the English. As he visualizes the design, he sees a "long line of shapes that resemble archers [who] let fly a cloud of arrows at the advancing Germans, who fall dead in their thousands."

French troops, their imaginations lubricated with *pinard* and *tafia*, were just as ready to credit the deity for their victory on the Marne. They spoke of finding dead Germans without visible wounds. Had they been scared to death by some terrifying vision? Others speculated about secret weapons. Lights had been reported in the sky over Paris, and thumps and bangs underground. The lights were traced to restaurants in Montmartre that ignored the blackout and neglected to turn off their advertising signs, while the subterranean noises came from cellar bakehouses where bakers thumped and pounded bread dough, the adulturants added to flour at government order having made it tougher to knead.

Unconvinced, *poilus* talked of Jules Verne-ian gadgets such as an invisible aircraft, the ancestor of today's drones, that could hover above the clouds and send down bolts of electricity to fry the enemy. Before the war, chemist Eugène Turpin, a friend of Verne and inspiration for at least one of his eccentric scientist characters, patented an improved explosive based on picric acid. Who was to know he didn't also develop a super shell that killed by displacement of air alone? He hadn't, and the troops learned in time that proximity to a conventional blast could be just as fatal. In April 1917, poet Edward Thomas survived the Battle of Arras, but stood up to light his pipe just as one of the last shells landed nearby. A second later he fell dead, but without a scratch.

The most resourceful wartime use of psychic phenomena took place not in Paris but in Turkey. Rather than waste troops as guards, the Turks trucked their prisoners hundreds of miles into the mountains, where an old farm in Yozgat Province became a prison camp. It required only a handful of guards. Any escapee would simply wander in the wilderness until he died of starvation and exposure.

Welshman Elias Jones and Australian C. W. Hill conceived an audacious plan. In nightly séances using a Ouija board and the type of verbal codes employed by vaudeville mind readers, they convinced, first their fellow prisoners, then the officers of the garrison that they could communicate with the spirit world. They told the commandant that the ghost of the farm's former owner, an Armenian killed by the Turks, had mentioned buried gold. Its location would be revealed only when the commandant had prayed for forgiveness at the grave of the murdered man. Jones and Hill intended to photograph the commandant as he did so, using a home-made camera. They would then blackmail him with the photos into setting them free. Wisely, they abandoned this crackpot scheme and simply mimed possession by evil spirits. It got them into hospital in Constantinople, from where they escaped or were released—ironically just a few weeks before the end of the war.

Jones and Hill were right to exploit the prevailing sense of madness. The war inspired a new belief that gods might intervene in the affairs of men: the Second Coming threatened in *The Land of Mist*. Those poets who survived the war were transformed by it. They no longer doubted the potency of the unseen. It perched on their shoulder, gibbering, sinking its claws into their flesh.

Robert Graves, in particular, turned away from the modern to embrace the muse of poetry, the White Goddess of Birth, Love, and Death. He related her to the deities of pagan mythology, and to the sybils, those psychics of the ancient world—prepubescent girls who, at Delphi, high above the Gulf of Corinth, perched on tripod seats over runnels of trickling water and, dazed by drug smoke and hormones, dispensed ambiguous advice to the emperors and satraps who abased themselves before them. Graves saw their era returning. "All a poet can do today is warn," wrote Wilfred Owen. Taking up the challenge, Graves used the poem "On Portents" to toll the alarm bell of dreadful times to come.

If strange things happen where she is,
So that men say graves open
And the dead walk, or that futurity
Becomes a womb and the unborn are shed,
Such portents are not to be wondered at,
Being tourbillions in Time made
By the strong pulling of her bladed mind
Through that ever-reluctant element.

35

The Beds in the West

Where is the home of love so dear?
Where but here—yea, here?
Here love and danger snatch the flower
Of life perchance a single hour,
Mate and die.
Here they lie—yea, here!
RUTH GAINES, "Paris 1917"

For almost a century, expatriate Paris had belonged, at least in culture, to the rich and educated. War alerted a much larger group to its pleasures. People moved there who would never have contemplated doing so before. Gertrude Stein wrote, "We saw a tremendous number of people but none of them as far as I can remember that we had ever known before. Paris was crowded. As Clive Bell [art historian and brother-in-law of Virginia Woolf] remarked, they say that an awful lot of people were killed in the war but it seems to me that an extraordinarily large number of grown men and women have suddenly been born."

One newcomer was songwriter Cole Porter, the lone contribution to American culture of Peru, Indiana. Notwithstanding having written a flop Broadway musical called *See America First*, Porter arrived in Paris in July 1917, supposedly to work for a war relief charity but actually to study composition with Vincent d'Indy at the Schola Cantorum. He later claimed to have taught gunnery to American soldiers at the French Officers School at Fontainebleau, and to have joined the recruiting department of American Aviation Headquarters. Other versions have him serving with the Foreign Legion in North Africa. In *Night and Day*, a deliciously ridiculous 1946 biopic starring Cary Grant, he's shown leaning against a palm tree, inspired by drums and some softly humming Zouaves to compose "Begin the Beguine" (actually written in 1935 during a Pacific cruise). In its obituary, the *New York Times* wrote, even less probably, that "he had a specially constructed portable piano made for him so that he could carry it on his back and entertain the troops in their bivouacs."

In a pungent and more accurate summary of Porter's Paris years, J. X. Bell wrote, "He made up stories about working with the French Foreign Legion and the French army. This allowed him to live his days and nights as a socialite and still be considered a 'war hero' back home. Paris parties during these years were elaborate and fabulous, involving people of wealthy and political classes. His were marked by much gay and bisexual activity, Italian nobility, cross-dressing, international musicians, and a large surplus of recreational drugs."

Another new arrival was Henry Sturgis Crosby of Back Bay, Boston, Massachusetts. The nephew of financier J. Pierpont Morgan, Crosby was tall, with startlingly good looks. He volunteered to drive an ambulance, and in November 1917 his vehicle took a near direct shell hit. "The hills of Verdun," he wrote deliriously of the experience and his survival, "and the red sun setting back of the hills and the charred skeletons of trees and the river Meuse and the black shells spouting up in columns along the road to Bras and the thunder of the barrage and the wounded and the ride through red explosions and the violent metamorphose from boy into man."

Unlike Hemingway, who survived a similar attack at the cost of shrapnel in his legs, Crosby was untouched—except, perhaps, psychologically. The moment he could leave the service, he moved to Paris and began squandering his trust fund on opium, alcohol, sex, religion—he founded his own cult, revering the sun—even publishing. His companion, Polly Peabody, renamed herself Caresse and acquired a whippet called Clitoris. Together, they founded the Black Sun Press, pioneering the published-in-Paris movement.

In 1929, returning to New York with his mistress, Crosby shot her in the head, then shot himself. He was thirty-one. *transition*, the magazine that published Joyce's *Finnegans Wake* and Hemingway's early stories, as well as Crosby's poems and photographs, ran an obituary by Kay Boyle. Her incoherence captured a sense of his fevered life but also that of Paris at war.

> *There was no one who ever lived more consistently in the thing that was happening then. If he crossed the sea, it was never a stretch he looked upon as wide rolling water, but every drop of it stung in him because he did not know how to keep things outside himself; every rotting bit of wreck in it was heaped on his own soul, and every whale was his own sporting, spouting young adventure. If he went into retreat, into his own soul he would go, trailing this clattering, jangling universe with him, this ermine-*

trimmed, this moth-eaten, this wine velvet, the
crown jewels on his forehead, the crown of thorns in
his hand, into retreat, but never into escape.

Not immune to the pleasures of Paris, even General Pershing enjoyed his creature comforts, living in a borrowed mansion with a garden at 73 rue de Varenne, close to the Hôtel des Invalides. It was there, as he awaited the first draft of troops, that he and his inner circle planned the United States' involvement in the war.

In their leisure hours, members of his staff, helped by their new acquaintances at the Union Interalliée, discovered fine dining and beautiful women. Harry Crosby's diaries offer a commentary on the pleasures of a Paris where, increasingly, old rules no longer applied. In a gesture toward its expanding international clientele, the city's most select brothel, La Chabanais, rebranded itself The House of All Nations. Crosby paid a visit, and gave his approval of "the Persian and the Russian and the Turkish and the Japanese and the Spanish rooms, and the bathroom with mirrored walls and mirrored ceilings, and the thirty harlots waiting in the salon."

The house prided itself on accommodating all tastes. Crosby saw "the flogging post where men came to flagellate young girls and where others (masochists) came to be flagellated." Voyeurs satisfied themselves in a room with peepholes. Men who enjoyed entering a vagina lubricated with the semen of another were invited to wait in a rear corridor until the first client left, then slip in. By special arrangement, fetishists could enjoy the latest in glamorous sexual sensations—a hot omelette slid sizzling from the pan onto their nude body.

The Crosbys also frequented an apartment on rue du Bois converted by a *rastaquouère* named Drosso into a luxurious *fumerie*. Caresse recalled "a series of small fantastic rooms, large satin divans heaped with pillows, walls covered with gold-embroidered arras, in the center of each room a low round stand on which was ranged all the paraphernalia of the pipe. By the side of each table, in coolie dress, squatted a little servant of the lamp. The air was sweet with the smell of opium." After they changed into kimonos, Harry sprawled on a couch with one arm around a beautiful French girl. Caresse snuggled under the other.

Drosso would cater private opium parties, bringing the drug to one's home, along with all the paraphernalia. Attractive *congees*, or servants, kept the pipes filled, as well as providing other services to any guests not wishing to enter what Baudelaire called the "artificial paradise" of drugged dreams.

To the French, one attraction of brothels and *fumeries* was the same as that of dinner parties: conversation. Men visited such places for the whole evening, or for days, and in some cases didn't sample the pleasures of the house at all. Lulled by the relaxed atmosphere, the drugs, and the company of beautiful women, gentlemen might exchange useful confidences, even secrets. Under the law that forbade pimping, only a woman could manage a *maison de tolérance*, but the actual proprietors were businessmen, politicians, even artists—Marcel Proust was part owner of two homosexual *maisons closes*—who recognized information as a commodity more precious than money.

Despite the execution of Mata Hari by a French firing squad in February 1917, nobody in Paris was unduly preoccupied with espionage. A wakeup call came toward the end of the year. Members of the American Field Service, including Hemingway, liked to gather at Harry's New York Bar on rue Danou, near the Opéra. Nobody suspected eavesdroppers, but in January 1918 the manager, a Monsieur Tepé, was arrested and interrogated by the security services. Later that day, he

"Black Jack" and "Papa"—Pershing and Joffre.

was found dead in the street below an open window. Evidently, more was going on behind the scenes than anyone suspected. Even then, nobody took such things very seriously. There was a general feeling that, with the Americans having tossed their hat in the ring, the whole business would be over by Christmas. Writing in

July, Albert Flament predicted, "The arrival of General Pershing will mark the definitive dispersal of those mists which, no matter when we looked, so heavily obscured our horizon." Who could have foreseen that peace was still more than a year away, and that the hardest was yet to come?

※ · 36 · ※

Machines

When the rich wage war, it's the poor who die.
JEAN-PAUL SARTRE

Throughout the early summer of 1917, as Pershing refined his strategy and, in England, at the opposite end of importance, Archie Baxter hobbled through a painful convalescence, the war crept closer to Paris.

Bombing raids increased, often now at night. During a dinner at the Ritz hosted by Paul Morand's fiancée and attended by the Beaumonts, Cocteau, and Proust, the lights went out. Morand wrote in his diary, "Searchlights in the starry skies from the direction of Le Bourget [military airfield]. Something like rockets; one by one the French planes climb up. Sirens wail." To break the tension, Cocteau joked, "Somebody's stepped on the toe of the Eiffel Tower, and it's complaining."

Roland Garros

A few nights after, at 10:00 p.m. on the evening of June 16, 1917, about twenty people gathered at Paul Morand's apartment above the colonnades of the Palais-Royale. They'd been invited to the first reading by Cocteau of his new cycle of poems, *Le Cap de Bonne-Espérance*.

The guest list was distinguished—not surprising, since he'd compiled it. The event took place "under the high patronage" of his old companion in arms (and pajamas) Etienne de Beaumont, and wife. Their presence was appropriate, since Cocteau's inspiration was the war: specifically, the war in the air. The poems were dedicated to his lover, the aviator Roland Garros, then a prisoner in Germany after having been shot down in Belgium. The *Stars and Stripes* published a harrowing account of his treatment in the prison camp at Küstrin.

> *This unfortunate had been led about with his*
> *hands tied, guarded by four men, one of whom*
> *was an officer, unbound only when his physical*
> *needs demanded, then forced to keep his arms*
> *in a horizontal position and made to sleep face*
> *downwards. While at Küstrin, an order came*
> *from Berlin that he should respond every two hours*
> *to roll-call, even during the night. This aviator,*
> *dragged from camp to camp, allowed only ten*
> *minutes' notice of departure, was submitted to*
> *such horrible torture that he asked the German*
> *government by letter to be shot.*

"Sultry," wrote Morand of the evening. "Not a breath of air; not a sound; under a lamp, Cocteau opens a notebook in which words in his large, naïve handwriting run on and jostle one another in keeping with to-day's aesthetic."

The poems saluted Garros and such aviators as Léon Morane, who invented the monoplane, with its unexpectedly thick and—to Cocteau's eyes—ungraceful single wing. To him, the ingenuity of such men recalled that of Napoleon, one of whose symbols, appropriately, was the industrious, often airborne bee.

The real subject of *Cap de Bonne-Espérance*, however, was the thrill of flight as experienced with Garros during their shared ascents. The opening of the cycle conveys Cocteau's breathless, almost incoherent wonder at a night flight over Paris.

> *Garros of you*
> *Garros here*
> *we*
> *You Garros*
> *Nothing else but black silence*

To Morand, the pauses and gaps evoked air pockets; moments when the sky no longer supported the flimsy plane and its daring pilot.

Seeing the world from the air was still novel enough for Cocteau to be impressed by aerial photographs shown to him by Garros at the military airport of Villacoublay. They included images of Malmaison, the château of Napoleon's wife, Joséphine de Beauharnais.

A lunch at Villacoublay
One sees in a stereoscope
All the photographs

Malmaison
The lawn Bees
The harp of Josephine
a thick
wing broken.

You lived in her room
Dear creole

With heavy tread, mechanized war was bearing down on Paris. In November, near Cambrai, the British and Australians experimented with a new strategy. Four hundred British tanks attacked German positions, preceded by a "creeping barrage" of artillery and followed by infantry. In theory, high explosives would annihilate the enemy in his trenches. Tanks would plow them down, and infantry mop up the few survivors.

Nothing worked as expected. The barrage was badly directed. Many shells fell short, some among the advancing infantry. Tanks got stuck in ditches or mired in mud. The infantry, expecting to find demoralized enemy troops, had to fight for their lives. The attack forced a bulge in the German line, but the Allies were soon back where they started, except for 179 tanks destroyed, and 55,207 dead or wounded, against the enemy's estimated 45,000.

Paris's café strategists shook their heads. After seeing a newsreel of tanks in action, Cocteau, noting the way they reared up at hitting an obstacle, compared them to "a safe that falls from the top floor of a house, then stands on its hind legs like a dog and begs a sugar cube." What next? Tanks and locomotives having sex, and giving birth to robot children?

For the first time, the war caused Cocteau to lose his temper. He raged against "this formless monster, which hops, flounders, tramples people in its clumsiness, eats them out of gluttony and vomits them right and left." Among those it devoured was Roland Garros, who escaped from Germany, only to be shot down at Vouziers in the Ardenne just a few days before the end of the war.

37

The Zouaves' Trousers

Yet all experience is an arch wherethrough
Gleams that untravelled world, whose margin fades
For ever and for ever when I move.
ALFRED, LORD TENNYSON, "Ulysses"

*O*n October 24, 1917, Archie Baxter set foot for the second time on French soil when he stepped off the boat in Le Havre.

Ships filled the vast ugly harbor: some standing out, waiting to dock; others moored, holds open, hatch covers off, cranes dipping into their guts, winches hauling out bulging cargo nets. Many boats were American. Black soldiers working as longshoremen offloaded crates onto the dock and wrestled them into railway trucks already coupled to locomotives leaking steam, ready to pull out.

Archie's experience of black men was limited to

Black French soldier guarding German prisoners

the few aboriginals who hung around the outskirts of Sydney, living in rough shelters, panhandling for cigarettes or beer. To him, these Americans were as exotic as flamingos; another promise of those different worlds he'd begun to glimpse the moment he made the decision to enlist.

It was still warm, the banked heat of autumn, so the Americans had stripped to the waist. They sang as they worked, the syncopated, repetitive chants of the slave life they hoped had ended with the Civil War. French stevedores handling cargo next to them took no notice. Recruits from the African colonies had made black skin even more of a commonplace. They sang too: tribal chants whose similarity to the Americans' work songs revealed their shared heritage.

Not that color made any difference to the French. Once they acknowledged you as *citoyen*, physical characteristics were of no significance. Whether a coolie from Cochin, a Zouave from Algeria, or a Spahi cavalryman from Morocco, you belonged to the culture of France, its art, its humor. When a Tommy wished to show skepticism, he might sneer, "Pull the other leg. It's got bells on." The *poilu*, to signify the ultimate in improbability, said, *"Oui. Et la main de ma soeur dans les culottes d'un zouave."* Sure. And my sister's hand in a Zouave's trousers.

After waiting in line for an hour at the routing office, Archie got a chit to spend the night in town.

"We'll send you up to the front with the next convoy," said the corporal behind the desk. "Might be a couple of days. Until we get together enough of you to make it worthwhile."

"Send us up where, corp?"

"None of your bloody business, mate. Report at HQ in town tomorrow. Next!"

With other Aussies off the same boat, Archie scrounged a lift into the center of town. The horse-drawn ambulance was returning empty after delivering wounded to a ship taking them back to Australia. The other new arrivals climbed into the back, under the canvas, finding room around the now-empty stretcher racks, but Archie, after one look at the bloody bandages littering the floor and a sniff of the mingled stink of disinfectant, unwashed bodies, and corruption, mounted the open front seat with the driver.

"G'day," he said.

"G'day," the driver replied.

As Australian etiquette went, it was a warm, even enthusiastic welcome.

The swaybacked chestnut pulling the ambulance made Archie realize how long it had been since he'd sat behind the complacent backside of a horse. Years. He hadn't missed it. Twenty years of living with a barnyard, and particularly with pigs, cured him of any affection for farm animals.

The road was solid with traffic, as far as the eye could see. Most of it horse-drawn: ambulances in one direction, many with casualties sitting next to the driver or cross-legged on top; in the other direction carts and trucks loaded with munitions, supplies, the nourishment of war.

European roads were not made for heavy traffic. Tall trees, mostly poplars, lined this one on both sides. Beyond, fields ran off into the distance, disappearing from sight in the mist that hung perpetually over Europe's plowed earth. Archie thought of Australia: the grass crisped brown, as if in an oven; the omnipresent hum of insects; the sky, white with heat; the sensation of sweat vaporizing on the skin. During a year in England, he'd forgotten what it was to be warm.

A dispatch rider on a motorbike roared down the center line between the two stationary lanes of traffic. Otherwise, nothing moved. After a few minutes, the driver put the reins down on the worn wooden seat and started to roll a cigarette. Sensing slackness, the horse twitched its head. Automatically Archie took the greasy leathers and tugged lightly. Reassured, the horse snorted and, without notice, dumped a load of turds onto the road.

Before they'd stopped steaming, Archie heard a scraping of spades below the wagon. Two kids in ragged hand-me-downs and wooden clogs were scooping the droppings into a bucket. Most houses had a manure heap filling the few square meters of space between the front wall and the ditch running along the edge of the road. This was still farmland, and fertilizer was wealth.

Striking a match on the wooden seat, the driver lit the cigarette, took a draw, then handed it to Archie. The smoke grated in his throat. Though the makings tasted only notionally of tobacco, he felt a diminishment of hunger and the beginnings of a buzz.

The driver nodded toward the ambulance halted on the opposite side of the road. The canvas was rolled back, probably to dissipate the smell that drove Archie up here to the front seat. Inside, as if in an insect nest, wounded men were exposed, swathed in bandages like larvae. Some lay silent and motionless on stretchers. Others lolled against bench seats. Some had their eyes bandaged; others a hand or foot.

"SIVs," the driver said.

"Eh?"

"Self-inflicted."

"How can you tell?"

"Haul enough of the buggers, you learn the signs."

"All of them?"

"Most. And more of 'em every week."

Every old stager had a recipe for a Blighty wound. The less imaginative blew off a toe or raised a hand above the parapet, hoping to be drilled by a German sniper without losing any fingers. Others ate the emetic ipecac or cordite from a rifle cartridge; it gave you shortness of breath and bad color, but it was easy to spot. A whiff or two of gas could burn your lungs or eyes badly enough to be invalided back but—with luck—do no permanent damage. An injection of petrol into the joint could make a knee or elbow swell, or, if under the skin, cause a nasty-looking ulcer. . . .

A powerful need to move seized Archie. He handed back the reins.

"Hoo-roo."

Startled, the man said, "If you want a jimmy riddle, go ahead. We're not moving."

"No, it's apples, mate. Good luck."

He shook the man's hand, dropped to the road and crossed to the other side, ignoring a horse that whinnied and showed its teeth, hoping for an apple or a carrot. Slithering down the embankment, he hopped the stagnant water in the ditch, filmed like a blind eye with algae, and scrambled up the other side. From the look of the few stalks of greenery mixed into the dug-over earth, the field had been under turnips until a few weeks ago.

Hands in his pockets, head pulled into the collar of his greatcoat, Archie wasn't sure he'd been spotted leaving the road—or, if he had, that anyone would care. The Allied forces were leaking people. He sensed them evaporating, the way a hot wind sucks away the liquid beaded on a canvas water bag. About the narrow raised bank between this field and the next, there was a quality of the foretold that steered him toward the line of trees about a quarter of a mile away; trees that could only mean one thing.

38

The Stars and Stripes Forever

Hurrah for the flag of the free!
May it wave as our standard forever,
The gem of the land and the sea,
The banner of the right.
JOHN PHILIP SOUSA,
"The Stars and Stripes March"

The poster and bookplate painted by Charles Buckles Falls for the War Service Library manages to be at the same time playful and martial. The doughboy wears a tin hat and carries a carbine, but the weapon is slung over his shoulder, and in flagrant defiance of all rules of safety, its bayonet is fixed. Not that he could use it in case of attack, since his arms

War Service Library bookplate

are filled with books, piled higher than his head. "This book," explains the text of the bookplate, "is provided by the people of the United States through the American Library Association for the use of the soldiers and sailors."

During the war, the American Library Association collected millions of books and shipped them to France. The library set up to distribute them still exists. Now the American Library in Paris, it's located in the tree-shaded seventh arrondissement, where at each street corner one encounters the Eiffel Tower peering inquisitively into your business.

These days, computer terminals are more evident than books at the ALP, and the emphasis less on reading than lap sits for toddlers and seminars on investment opportunities, with a free glass of boxed Beaujolais afterward. But its complacency is less a sign of senescence than of success. The battle has long since been won. Large parts of twenty-first-century Paris have become as American as *tarte aux cerises*.

*I*n retrospect, the American force sent to help the Allies in 1917 was an invading army as well. Europe, already half converted to an Americanized way of life by its seductive popular culture, and deeply in debt to its money men, was ready to embrace, as its avant-garde had already done, a world inhabited by Buffalo Bill, Pearl White, and Charlie Chaplin, in which one drank martinis and old-fashioneds, drove a Ford, snapped pictures with a Kodak, wound up a Victor gramophone, and danced the one-step and *le fox* to the music of James Reese Europe.

If one could specify a single moment in which Paris surrendered to that seduction, it came in August 1918.

Finally, Paris felt it could exhale the breath it had been holding for three years. The *Paris-Geschütz*, its usefulness at an end, had been hauled back to Germany. On the Amiens front, on the Marne, and in the Saint-Mihiel salient, the Germans were in retreat. Not so much because of the war news as the fact that it was the sort of thing one did in August, Etienne and Edith de Beaumont threw a garden party in their eighteenth-century town house at 2 rue Duroc.

The occasion was the premier performance of a work by young Francis Poulenc, a piece for baritone and piano quintet plus flute and clarinet, called *La Rapsodie Nègre*.

Its inspiration was the music for *Parade*. Poulenc was an admirer of Satie, to whom the piece was dedicated.

The title tipped a wink at jazz and Africa, but the piece was actually a spoof—a setting of a poem by "Liberian poet Makoko Kangourou," a name which, like the text—*Honoloulou, poti lama!/honoloulou, honoloulou,/ kati moko, mosi bolou,* etc.—was patently fake.

The words were probably influenced by the "boom-lay boomlay boomlay BOOM" and "Mumbo-Jumbo will hoo-doo you" of Vachel Lindsay's poem "The Congo," published in 1914 and subtitled "A Study of the Negro Race." In turn, Scott Fitzgerald may have been harking back to this event when he had the band at Jay Gatsby's party present "Vladimir Tostoff's *Jazz History of the World* that created a sensation at Carnegie Hall last year."

By 1914, the heavy artillery of American cinema and popular music had already softened up the Europeans. After 1918, Hollywood would buy up the remains of the German and French film industries and stake a claim to the British. In 1925, it absorbed France's design expertise as well by copying and merchandizing art deco, which France had introduced to the world at its Exposition Internationale des Arts Décoratifs et Industriels Modernes.

But for the moment, the front on which it fought was

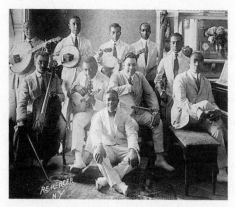

James Reese Europe and musicians

jazz. James Reese Europe, chosen to form and lead the band of the 369th Infantry Regiment, the Harlem Hellfighters, had been a club owner in Harlem, a composer, and musical director for the exhibition dancers Vernon and Irene Castle. In France, his musicians traveled over two thousand miles, performing for British, French, and American military audiences as well as French civilians. They also made recordings for Pathé, planting the seed of jazz that would germinate after 1920 in the soil of France.

Following Europe's death in 1919, stabbed in a trivial skirmish with a drummer in his band, a mourner said, "Before Jim Europe came to New York, the colored man knew nothing but Negro dances and porter's work. All that has been changed. Jim Europe was the living open sesame to the colored porters of this city. He took them from their porters' places and raised them to positions of importance as real musicians." Just as importantly, he alerted them to the opportunities, social and musical, of France. Numerous African American performers who remained in Paris after the war or returned following their demobilization were living proof that he was right.

The American Library retains a few relics of its early years. One of them, an unwieldy bound volume, sits awkwardly in the sleek glass and aluminum decor. A librarian and an old friend, Simon Gallo, climbs a ladder to bring it down from exile on top of a shelf unit.

Multilingual, a collector of seventeenth-century bindings, Simon lived in Brazil and Italy before coming to Paris, He belongs to the same scholarly brotherhood as Neil in London and Peter van Diemen.

"We don't get many requests for this," he says as he helps me carry the book to a table in the reading room.

"I can tell."

The yellowing newsprint is fragile. With too much exposure to light and incautious hands, the pages would become brittle and crumble, like an ancient scroll or papyrus.

Pershing had been in France only eight months when the first number appeared of the forces' weekly newspaper, *Stars and Stripes*. Its staff included Harold Ross, who would go on to found and edit *The New Yorker* magazine; the future columnist Franklin P. Adams; sports journalist Grantland Rice; and Alexander Woollcott, destined to tramp like a wounded elephant through American culture as theater critic, humorist, playwright, and model for the irascible Sheridan Whiteside in *The Man Who Came to Dinner*.

Stars and Stripes ran until June 1919, its pages a priceless record not so much of war news—censorship restricted that—as of the preoccupations of the Americans who read and edited it. Foremost among these was food. None of the Allies took to French food—which, in any event, was difficult to find close to the front line. The restaurant-bars called *estaminets* learned that *rosbifs* and *kangourous* were not adventurous eaters. Rather than explaining French cuisine, it was easier to offer something they all enjoyed—fried eggs and chips. Patrons seldom complained, except about the price.

Americans were even more attached to their national diet. Under the headline "Cigarettes Are Here," *Stars and Stripes* reported:

At bases in France there are 200,000,000 cigarettes
waiting for transportation to haul them to the
front. The Army recently commandeered a large
percentage of the YMCA's motor trucks. Here are
some things for the Army to be delivered to the
YMCA in France next month; 77 tons of chewing
gum, 1325 tons of flour and 2850 pounds of sugar
for cookie making, 167 tons of chocolate bars, 200
tons of jam, 94 tons of condensed milk, 31 tons of
cough drops, 176 tons of chewing tobacco, 9 tons of
plain soap, 17 tons of tooth paste, 6 tons of towels,
1½ tons of razor blades and 7 tons of playing cards.

Colonial powers rely on converting subject races to
their own values, teaching them the national language,
introducing them to the national cuisine, educating
them in the national manners. It would take a while for
the French to realize that the Americans had no inten-
tion of becoming French. Rather, they intended to turn
the French into Americans. Over the next century, the
two cultures would fight each other to a standstill.

But it was becoming clear that four years of war and
exposure to alien standards had damaged France as much
as the American Civil War wounded the United States.
Of the war's effect on France, Edith Wharton wrote,

"Like a monstrous landslide, it had fallen across the path of an orderly laborious nation, disrupting its routine, annihilating its industries, rending families apart, and burying under a heap of senseless ruin the patiently and painfully wrought machinery of civilization."

Gertrude Stein coined the phrase "lost generation" to describe not the disillusioned expatriate writers, but those young French men and women who, because of the war, hadn't finished their education, learned a trade, or developed an affinity for their culture. When, after 1919, Paris was gripped by *les années folles*, the crazy years, many of the disaffected young would find work in the growth industries of show business, prostitution, and crime.

No longer the woman of Europe, Paris became its whore, the international capital of sex and jazz, jiving to the charleston, the black bottom, *le fox*. Cafés rebranded themselves as *bars americains*, serving the cocktails the French never drank. High-stakes casinos, banished in 1913 beyond a hundred-kilometer radius of the city, returned now as spurious "clubs." One of the largest, the Sporting Club de France, bought a mansion next to the residence of the president, installed a gym and a swimming pool, then dropped the pretence. "Members mostly 'sport' in the card rooms," noted journalist Basil Woon, "and days go by when the pool is empty of anything but water."

The arrival of Prohibition in 1920 would accelerate the flow of tourists. Visiting Paris for the first time in 1906, Ezra Pound met people who'd never seen an American. After the war, they could scarcely be avoided. By 1923, 135,000 arrived there every year, a number rising fast. So devalued would the franc become that, as Ernest Hemingway explained in a 1923 article for *Esquire*, one could live comfortably in Paris for a year on just a thousand U.S. dollars.

One historian analyzed these changes optimistically as "a giant step into modernity. Life would never again be about a state of being; it would be about *doing*. Pleasure would give way to productivity, and men who were once worshipped for their beauty, money, and abundance of leisure time would become extraneous when usefulness and purpose took over."

Painters, composers, and authors were not so philosophical. Accustomed to singing for their supper at the salons of the rich, they would find those tables bare, their candles snuffed, the gas lamps dimmed, never to be relit. In the electric light that illuminated postwar Paris, a culture that looked its best in the soft glow of gas and beeswax was exposed by the pitiless glare of the incandescent bulb as blighted and sick to death.

39

The City of Darkness

*As a small boy, I felt in my heart two contradictory feel-
ings, the horror of life and the ecstasy of life.*
CHARLES BAUDELAIRE,
My Heart Laid Bare, 1887

Archie woke to a nudge in his ribs. He barely felt
it through the greatcoat wrapped around him,
but a second dig, more of a kick, opened his eyes. The
bargeman's wife, half-crouched, was staring down at
him through the open hatch, a blob of darker darkness
against a sky without stars.

"Nous voilà."

Archie boosted himself onto the deck. He could have
slept warm in the cabin, but as he was, technically at
least, AWOL, it seemed more prudent to doss down on
some empty sacks in the hold, which, during the down-

river part of the trip, had held cabbages. Their gassy smell hung around him as he shivered in the predawn chill, sensing rather than seeing buildings lining both sides of the river.

This was Paris? At 3:00 a.m., and obscured by the blackout, it looked desolate, abandoned. Then a light flared on the bank. A man in a flat cap, pushing a bicycle, had paused to light a cigarette. As he cupped the match to his mouth, his face seemed to float in velvet blackness. For an instant he looked across at Archie, probably seeing no more than a shrouded shape bulking against the loom of the dark. The spark of his discarded match arced into the water. Archie almost thought he heard it hiss.

At the same moment, the barge angled toward the opposite bank. So deep was the silence of the sleeping city that he heard the gurgle of the water under its bow. Other barges lined the bank, moored to iron bollards and rings sunk into the stone abutment. On the deck of one, wet shirts and underwear hung limp from a line; another had a rowboat lashed to the stern. Archie glimpsed a window, with a flowerpot, a wilting tulip.

"*Allez. Allez vite!*"

As the gap narrowed, he hopped across the few feet of black water onto the moored barge, then, carried by his momentum, across its deck and onto the bank. By the time he looked back, the barge that brought him up from Le Havre was barely visible. Before he could wave his thanks, it had disappeared altogether.

Fifty yards ahead, an old stone bridge loomed. He walked under its arch, through a miasma of rotting damp and ancient piss. Something scuttled in the dark. Rats. But on the other side, stone steps led up to street level.

He emerged next to the statue of a man on a horse; what man it was too dark to tell, since the dim orange streetlights barely lit the pavement. But probably some king; it usually was.

He looked around at the deserted streets with a sense of anticlimax. His spontaneous gesture of independence now looked absurd. He felt like the general who, ready to surrender, could find nobody to accept his sword.

A horse-drawn cart materialized out of the dark and clopped toward him. But nobody sat on the high bench seat. Where was the driver? Only as it passed did he notice a figure lying on top of the load, reins wrapped round his hands, apparently asleep.

A pothole jolted the cart and something fell off. Stepping out into the street, Archie picked it up. A carrot. Realizing he was hungry, and taking the vegetable as Paris's offhand gift of welcome, a sort of key to the city, he wiped it on the side of his coat and took a bite, the earth grating on his teeth.

As he chewed, another cart approached. He felt through the stones rather than heard the heavy tread of the hooves, the iron wheels grinding the cobbles. Materializing from the same direction as the first, it crossed in front of him, close enough for him to see the tousled hair of the boy on top, his blond hair like a more refined sketch of the heads of cauliflowers on which he slept.

Sustained by the carrot juice, Archie stepped into the road and joined the somnambulistic caravan.

He heard and smelled the market before he saw it: a muted muttering of voices and noise, carried on the same waft as the cocktail of odors—fruit, meat, herbs, smoke—that shouted in the universal language of appetite: "Food."

By the time he could see the vast iron-and-glass pavilions, glowing like lanterns in the dark, he was walking alongside a score of carts, nose to tail. Sensing the lack of motion, farm boys were awaking sleepily, unrolling themselves from their cocoon-like woolen coats. Hand-knitted on thick needles, they used wool that retained the original grease. It waterproofed the garment, at the cost of making the wearer smell like a sheep.

A few boys hung feed bags over the heads of the

horses. One, taking a leisurely piss in the gutter, nodded as Archie walked past.

The head of the line was a melée of disciplined activity. Brawny men in ankle-length aprons led horses to where others with baskets and handcarts waited to offload turnips, potatoes, cabbages, kale, onions, and other vegetables Archie had never seen, let alone eaten. Everything was hauled into the nearest pavilion, where avenues of market stalls disappeared into the remote distance.

To left and right, other carts at other pavilions disgorged baskets of apples and pears or sides of lamb and pork. Men in bloody aprons balanced whole carcasses on their heads. Others hauled heavy handcarts loaded with produce. And everywhere, a torrent of noise and an avalanche of odors.

Among the sounds and smells, he identified some that interested him most. They came not from the market but from cafés that lined the streets. One at the next corner, larger and brighter than the others, displayed a sign over the door. LE CHAT QUI FUME. The cat that . . . fumes? A painting on one of its windows, of a ragged tabby with a pipe, provided the clue. The Smoking Cat.

A big red car nosed into the street behind him, its driver hooting at the queued-up carts. Nobody took any notice. Finally, it rode its front wheels up onto the sidewalk, and the passengers, five of them, dressed in evening clothes, climbed out. As they pushed through the double doors into the restaurant, their chauffeur got out, tilted his cap with the shiny visor onto the back of his head, and, leaning against the mudguard, lit a cigarette.

Archie followed the party into the café.

Even at three in the morning, the place was seething. For all the notice they took of the world outside, it might have been bright day and not the middle of the night. Waiters in long aprons wove between the tables, holding trays above their heads loaded with glasses of beer and wine and plates of food. There was a constant traffic of people climbing and descending a wooden staircase to the first floor. The roar of conversation blended into a fog of sound as all-enveloping as the mixture of cigarette smoke and breath and food smells that passed for air.

A couple got up from a tiny corner table, and Archie seized it, wedging himself against the wall. He'd begun to sweat, but it was too late now to struggle out of his greatcoat. Resigning himself to discomfort, he looked around the room.

The party from the car were installed in the corner opposite, spreading out over two tables. The women, shrugging their evening cloaks off bare shoulders of ivory and gold, let the rich, brilliantly figured fabric spill across the back of their chairs, even brush the floor. As one of them crossed her legs, a slim ankle enclosed in a silver sandal emerged from a shimmer of electric blue satin.

The three men were in evening dress, but one of them—the undoubted star—also wore a light beige overcoat, which he didn't remove; just left it draped like a cloak over his narrow shoulders. Though he should be perspiring like Archie, he was not a man with whom one associated the word "sweat." Thin and pale, with a narrow birdlike face, he never stopped talking or moving his thin pale hands. They fluttered.

"Je vous écoute."

A waiter stood over Archie, staring indifferently through the window toward the market.

"Uh . . . I don't know."

The man at the next table, one of the market porters, was spooning up soup covered with a cheesy crust. Archie pointed to it.

"This."

"D'acc. Soupe à l'oignon," the waiter said, making a note. *"Et pour boire?"*

Seeing that Archie didn't understand, he frowned in exasperation, then mimed upending a glass.

"Uh . . . beer?"

"Bière." The waiter left, yelling over his shoulder, in the direction of the bar, *"Un pression!"*

"Puis-je m'asseoir ici?"

The girl just materialized. He hadn't seen her come in—wondered later if she might have been upstairs and seen him from the stairs. Old or young, pretty or plain? Under the rice powder, lipstick, and mascara, the fringe of black hair, he received only that instinctive animal impression of Other.

"I . . . uh, I don't . . . I mean . . ."

"Ah, English?"

"No. Australian."

"Australien . . . huh." She touched the back of the chair opposite. "I can?"

"Yes. Please. Sit."

She sat, and put a purse—cracked black patent leather, clasp rubbed down to the yellow brass—on the table next to her hand.

"You are army? *En permission?*"

He shook his head. "I don't speak . . ."

"Permission is . . ." She searched for the English word. "Leave?"

"Oh, yes. Leave."

She mimed smoking; two fingers to her lips. "Cigarette?"

"I don't . . ." He thought of the cat with the pipe. *"Fume."*

"Ah, *vous parlez français."*

He shook his head. "But you *parlez anglais."*

Her pout signified doubt or disagreement.

"Little . . . Enough . . ." A seesaw motion with her hand. "Not enough. *Alors* . . ." Her eyes moved around the room restlessly. "So . . . no cigarette. A drink?"

"Yes. If you like. What?"

Casually she reached behind her, snagged a waiter with a hand on his arm and spoke very fast. He nodded and shouted something to the barman. Belatedly, Archie remembered horror stories of men on leave lured into bars where girls ordered expensive drinks and forced them to pay.

She seemed to sense his panic.

"Du calme. Is not champagne. A *pastis."* She held out her hand to shake. "Edith." She didn't pronounce the "h" so it came out "Ay-dit."

He took her fingers in his. "Archie."

"Achille?"

"No. Arch-*ee.*"

She tried again, but the "ch" defeated her.

"All right," he said. *"Achille."* Could anyone really

take him for an Achilles? But the very thought made him feel bolder.

The corner party had become more animated, the man with the pale hands more voluble. With the coat over his shoulders, he resembled a gaunt desert bird with folded wings.

She followed his gaze. "You know?"

"Me? No. Do you?"

She stared over her shoulder, frankly inquisitive. The second of the two women, small, dark, was talking, leaning forward, moving her head. Diamonds sparkled at her ears.

When Edith turned back, she said, "Her, I think. The Jew. *Une comtesse de Hongrie, je crois.*" Seeing that Archie didn't understand, she went on, "The *brune* . . . dark hair. A countess, I think. Of . . . 'ungary?"

The waiter brought his beer and her *pastis*, with a jug of water.

"And the man? With the coat?"

"Uh . . . *moment*. I listen." Abstractedly, her attention focused on the conversation at the other table, she trickled water into the glass as she did so. As if watching a magic trick, Archie saw the green liquid become suddenly milky.

At last she said, "I think . . . writer?" She listened some more. "He talk about . . ."

Exasperated, she buttonholed their waiter again. After a muttered conversation, she let him go and turned back to Archie.

" 'is name Jean Cocteau. 'E write *poésie, pièce théâtrale* . . . er, play for theater. Is *pedé* . . ." She made the universal gesture of the limp wrist. "How do you say?"

"We say 'poofter'—but I know what you mean."

"Pouf-tair?" She grinned. "*Chouette!* My first Australian word!"

The waiter plonked down Archie's soup, a spoon, and a napkin. Just the smell was enough to make him salivate.

He gestured to Edith. "Would you . . . ?"

She shook her head and tapped her glass with one nail.

As he ate, she listened to the man she called Cocteau and gave Archie a running commentary.

" 'E talk of zer war. (*Everyone* talk of war. I am *tired* of zis war.) 'E lose, 'e say, seven friends . . . one, *un poète*, Apollinaire. . . . Ah, I 'ave seen this one in here. Fat . . ." She mimed winding something around her head. "*Blessé.*"

Some gestures were universal. A bandaged head wound.

But she was listening again.

"Another . . . *un aviateur* . . . oh, Garros! Was friend of Garros."

Archie found he could reconstruct much of what the man was saying just from watching his hands. Turned toward the others, palms outward, offering, *I don't have to tell you, my friends.* . . . Palms inward, crossed on his chest, *My heart, my very soul* . . . The right hand lifted, open, with a gesture of release, *Gone* . . . The same hand laid like a dead thing on the table, *Never to return. . .*

But then he made a gesture Archie couldn't read. The hands lifted, turned outward as if to encompass the whole of existence: the long face morose, chin high, a slow shake of the head, the eyes close to tears. Christ, sorrowing for the fall of Man.

"What's he saying?"

"Oh . . . is *poésie. N'importe.*"

"No. Please. What?"

She sighed. " 'E talk of Paree. *Un cité des ténèbres.* A city of . . . dark shadows? 'E look for *verité* . . . truth." That moue again, now signifying skepticism. "Is *poésie. Ca ne fait rien.*"

His soup bowl was empty. The beer glass too. Apparently he'd eaten and drunk both, though he couldn't remember doing so. The girl's *pastis* was gone also.

Delving inside his uniform, he found his meager roll of notes and started to peel off the largest. Shaking her head, Edith took the money, selected three notes of smaller denomination, and handed back the rest.

"Save . . . for hotel."

"No hotel. I came . . ." Unable to explain the complexities of his flight, he fell back on French usage, and shrugged.

She pointed at the money in his hand. "For hotel . . . is not much. For *good* hotel . . ." She shook her head. Her expression conveyed her opinion of the kind of room he could get for this kind of money.

Looking at him appraisingly, she teased out another note between thumb and forefinger.

"For Edith?"

"Yes. Why not?"

She smiled and made another *moue*. This time, a fake kiss.

"You come," she said, standing up.

"Come . . . where?"

"*Chez moi*. Is *salle de bain*." She wrinkled her nose.

"You smell of *choux* . . . cabbage." She hooked her arm through his. "And you will tell me of *les kangourous*."

They walked out into the morning, past Cocteau, who was still talking to his spellbound friends.

Paris didn't seem like a city of darkness to Archie.

It seemed wonderful.

*B*ut . . . it never happened!" said Peter van Diemen.
"It *might* have."

"Well, anything *might* have. But where's your evidence?"

"Cocteau was in Paris. He went to places like *Le Chat Qui Fume* with Morand and other friends. . . ."

"But we don't know that your grandfather was ever even in Paris. Let alone that he met Cocteau."

"I'm not saying he *met* him."

Peter's expression showed how little he thought of such hair-splitting. "You can't simply invent things."

"How do you account for his behavior then? The decision to volunteer. The fascination with Paris. The refusal to return to his wife."

"I don't have an explanation. A few speculations, perhaps."

"Like what?"

"Well . . ." He laid a postcard on the table. "This was in the documents you gave me."

The photo side showed a naked baby, facedown on a rug. I turned it over. Someone had written in a studied, looping hand, "To My Daling Dady From his Darling little daughter Stella Baxter 74 Catherine St Leichhardt June 10th 1917 Send me a big doll dad." It was addressed simply "Private W A Baxter on active Service abroad."

"This must be my aunt then," I said. "Dad's little sister. We always called her Mary."

I tried to square this infant with the bulky lady who'd been a fixture of my childhood and adolescence.

"Do you know when she was born?" van Diemen asked.

"No idea. From the look of this card, about 1916."

"1917. February 6, to be precise."

"So?"

"This would mean that, assuming a normal pregnancy, she was conceived in May of 1916. Archie volunteered in May 1916."

"Meaning . . . ?"

"Getting your wife pregnant doesn't suggest a man who wanted to cut all ties with his family. Quite the reverse, in fact. He would have sailed in October knowing she was expecting."

He sorted through the papers.

"Another thing . . . I found this."

It was a smudged copy of a three-line death notice from a newspaper.

BAXTER. June 2, 1913, at his parents' residence, 11 Catherine-street, Leichhardt, Claude Hector Robert, dearly-loved infant son of Mr. and Mrs. Archie Baxter, aged 5 weeks. "A bud In heaven."

"The house number is wrong."

"How many Archie Baxters can there be on one street?"

"So my grandfather lost a son, almost at birth?"

"Not one. Three." Another paper. "This is his death certificate. He was sixty-one. Cause of death— auricular fibrillation, myocarditis, and hypertension. And look; under 'children of the marriage,' it lists John, your father; Neville, your uncle; and Stella Mary, your aunt, as living and '3 males, deceased.'"

He laid his hand on the papers.

"You know what I see here? A man who suffered a great deal of loss. Three sons dead in infancy. From what you say, a difficult domestic situation. A job he didn't like. I see a man with a tendency to high blood pressure; probably inclined to mood swings; not an easy man to get on with."

"My cousins tell me the same thing. My father too. He had to move away from home as a boy, to live with another family."

"Some men respond to stress and loss by remaining and accepting. Some grieve and brood. Some run away. I would guess Archie belonged to that last group. He left his father's farm for the city. He left his wife for France . . ."

"And when he came back, he left her again, to try running his own business."

"I found out something about that too. You said he made condiments? Remember the branch of your family that set up a successful business in Scotland making canned goods and preserves? Look at this."

It was a printout from the Wikipedia entry for the Baxter company.

Baxters is an international food company, based in Fochabers, Moray, Scotland. It has its roots in a grocer's shop opened by George Baxter in 1868. Baxter's shop became known for supplying pickles

and preserves in the early 20th century, when
Baxter's son and daughter-in-law began preparing
their own beetroot and selling it to other grocers.

"Pickles and preserves. Not far from condiments."

I remembered that someone told me Archie made very good pickled onions.

"You think he was trying to repeat what his . . . uncle? cousin? . . . achieved?"

"Don't you think it's possible?"

"Yes, it's *possible*. But what about *la cité des ténèbres* and *San fairy ann*?"

"Things he read. Things he heard. Who knows? Every life is a mystery. Sometimes one has to embrace the inexplicable."

When I got home, I walked out on our terrace and looked across the roofs of Paris toward Notre Dame.

Archie had never lived in France. But here I was, two generations later, with a French wife and daughter and an apartment in the heart of Paris—a city in which I had never meant to settle but to which I had been drawn from the other side of the world.

Drawn by what? A gene? A fragment, lodged somewhere in the genetic record, of my grandfather's need for another and better life in a country far from his own?

I might never know what Archie hoped to find in Paris or what he had found here. If it was to forget his life and family, to start again as his own man, he had come to the wrong place. In the city of Cocteau and Proust, the past was as real as the present. This is a city that remembered. Far from rejecting pain, it embraced it, transformed it. I loved it for that—loved it as one preserves the memory of lost loves and remembers with nostalgia rather than regret the illusions of youth. I loved it as had Rimbaud. He spoke for all us newcomers when he wrote in "The Drunken Boat":

If there is one water in Europe I want, it is the
Black cold pool where into the scented twilight
A child squatting full of sadness, launches
A boat as fragile as a butterfly in May.

❋ · ACKNOWLEDGMENTS · ❋

Our family is typical in having preserved too little of its past. What has been saved is due to the efforts of my brother, Philip, and my sister, Virginia, without whom it would not have been possible to write this book. Thanks are also due to Robyn Lopes, my cousin on my mother's side, for her meticulous documentation.

In London, Mary Troath was, as always, the most creative and indefatigable of researchers. I'm grateful to Neil Hornick for the generous access to his archives and for his cordial elucidation of the complexities of British society. In Australia, Michael Caulfield was unstinting with his time, expertise, and friendship. I'm particularly grateful to the Australian War Memorial and the National Archives of Australia, Canberra, for assistance and advice. In Paris, Dr. Barbara Santich, by inviting me to her lecture at the Australian embassy in Paris, brought this book a giant step closer to fruition. Simon

Gallo at the American Library in Paris kindly arranged access to its files of *Stars and Stripes*. Thanks to my longtime editor at HarperCollins, Peter Hubbard, and to my agent, Jonathan Lloyd. I'm also grateful to the many others at Harper who have labored on my behalf, among them: Cole Hager, Amy Baker, Cal Morgan, Milan Bozic, Julie Hersh, Fritz Metsch, Gregory Henry, and Sarah Woodruff. And to "Peter van Diemen," as he prefers to be known, my most heartfelt thanks. *Ein Gespenst ist noch wie eine Stelle, dran dein Blick mit einem Klange stößt.*

INDEX

Page numbers in *italics* refer to illustrations.

John Baxter has lived in Paris for more than twenty years. He is the author of four acclaimed memoirs about his life in France: *The Perfect Meal: In Search of the Lost Tastes of France*; *The Most Beautiful Walk in the World: A Pedestrian in Paris*; *Immoveable Feast: A Paris Christmas*; and *We'll Always Have Paris: Sex and Love in the City of Light*. Baxter, who gives literary walking tours through Paris, is also a film critic and biographer whose subjects have included the directors Fellini, Kubrick, Woody Allen, and most recently, Josef von Sternberg. Born in Australia, he lives with his wife and daughter in the Saint-Germain-des-Prés neighborhood, in the same building Sylvia Beach called home.